Preston
Buses

Mike Rhodes

'This book is dedicated to the memory of Preston Bus Depot Engineer
Jim Hilton (1947-2013) who died suddenly on 21st August 2013'

© 2014 Mike Rhodes and Venture Publications Ltd

ISBN 9781905304554

Contents

Introduction	3
Acknowledgements	3
1. Tram and Bus Developments to 1968	5
2. Fleet Standardisation	25
3. De-regulation and Privatisation	36
4. Stagecoach and Rotala	53
5. Liveries and Destination Equipment	75
6. Rebuilds and Modifications	91
7. Depot Developments	103
Buses Operated 1922-2013	107
Services Operated	110
Trams operated 1904-1935	111
Preston Area Map	112

Title Page
One of the defining decisions made by the Transport Committee was the one made in 1974 to embark on a rolling programme of fleet modernisation based on the Atlantean chassis. Between 1975 and 1983 the fleet became almost entirely based on the type as successively they replaced the last 20 PD2s and all of the PD3s and Panthers. Eventually numbering 79 vehicles, 20 carried Alexander AL type bodywork whilst the remainder all had East Lancashire built bodies. The last of the type were not withdrawn until 2007. Alexander-bodied No.109 is seen outside the Continuation Hospital in Midgery Lane on 24th August 1980. When new, the first 40 had the little box at the front which when illuminated proclaimed 'Pay on Entry' as the type were initially used on both 'PAYB' and crew operated services. Nos. 102/4-7/10 all later received the Derek Fullerton treatment when they were rebuilt at the front after sustaining accident damage. No.109 was sold to Hyndburn Borough Transport in November 1990 and converted to single doorway. It subsequently passed to Stagecoach Ribble in 1997 but is reported to have been scrapped a couple of years later.

Introduction

The city of Preston lies to the north of the river Ribble and was once renowned for its cotton trade and heavy industry. At the sprawling English Electric Co Works in Strand Road, trams, buses and railway locomotives were built and exported to destinations all over the world. Adjacent to the E E Co Works was the large dock complex, which was a busy port during most of the twentieth century through to the late 1960s when an irreversible decline set in, leading to closure in 1981. Preston has always had good transport links and is situated on the main London to Glasgow railway line. In the 1950s and 1960s tens of thousands of holidaymakers passed through the town by road and rail on their way to the Lancashire resorts of Blackpool and Morecambe. Traffic congestion is nothing new and the Arterial Road (Blackpool Road) used to be solid with nose to tail traffic. This was the catalyst for the construction of the Preston by-pass which was opened in 1958 and was the first section of motorway to be built in the country and now forms part of the busy M6.

Preston's first railed local transport service was a horse drawn tram route which was inaugurated on 20th March 1879 and ran from the town centre to Fulwood. Other horse tram routes soon followed and these maintained the local services until the end of 1903. Preston Corporation built a depot complex and generating station in Deepdale Road and commenced operations with thirty electric trams, all of which had been built in the town, on 7th June 1904. The tram network was expanded and continued to exclusively serve the townsfolk until January 1922 when the first bus route was introduced. In July 1932 the first tram routes were converted to motorbus operation and by the end of 1935 the trams were no more and all the town's services were in the hands of motorbuses. Despite obtaining the necessary powers in 1931 to operate trolleybuses, it was the bus fleet which expanded as routes were opened up to more areas of the town.

In 1966 the fleet livery was changed from maroon and cream to blue and ivory and variations of these colours still feature in the present day livery. 'Pay-as-you-board' buses were introduced in December 1968 and the last conductors were finally retired in 1982. Bus de-regulation took place in 1986 and the undertaking had to fend off stiff competition from United Transport Ltd before becoming a limited company seven years later, when it was bought out by the management and employees. Competition again followed but nothing was to prepare Preston Bus for the bitter battle which ensued with Stagecoach, from June 2007. Not surprisingly the company couldn't compete on equal terms and sold out to Stagecoach in January 2009. Almost immediately the purchase was referred to the Competition Commission and their report decreed that Stagecoach must divest itself of the company. Enter Rotala, who re-established a local brand and put the company back on an even keel.

In 2002 Preston was bestowed city status and this is reflected in the text as the story unfolds. The early history of the undertaking has previously been covered by the author in 'Preston's Trams and Buses' published by Venture Publications in 1995 and is therefore not described in the same detail in this account. Preston is well known for several reasons. One of the finest footballers ever to play the game, Sir Tom Finney, was born and bred in the city and only ever played professional football for his home town club of Preston North End. Often quoted is the phrase 'Once every Preston Guild' which refers to the Town's/City's celebrations which are held every twenty years. The history of the undertaking spans five Guilds, namely those held in 1922, 1952, 1972, 1992 and 2012. In the past the undertaking has always had a large part to play in ensuring the celebrations during Guild week pass off as smoothly as possible. The 2012 Guild proved to be no different and was fully embraced by Rotala.

Today Rotala operate much of the city's route network and whilst the Bus Station, which at one time was under the threat of demolition, has now been reprieved, Rotala are looking to move to new garage premises in the not too distant future.

Mike Rhodes January 2014

Acknowledgements

The author would like to thank employees and management past and present at Preston Bus for continued access to the depot premises and for information provided over the last forty years or so, without which this account would not have been possible. The author would also like to acknowledge the use of the PSV Circle publication PC28 as a source of invaluable information and the various photographers whose material has been used to illustrate the book.

The tram tracks are still in situ outside Miller Arcade as relatively new English Electric-bodied Leyland TD2 No. 46 waits to leave for Farringdon Park whilst No. 49 of the same batch is seen behind on the Ribbleton R service. This batch of TD2s were the first tram replacement buses which entered service in July 1932.

In 2012 the now Rotala-owned Preston Bus received seven new hybrid Optare Versas which replaced a similar number of Solos which dated from 2002. Whilst Nos. 30123-5 were dedicated to the Capitol Centre Park & Ride service, the remaining four were predominantly to be seen on service 19. 30131 was initially given the number 30128 and it is seen in the Guild Trades Procession on 1st September 2012.

1. Tram and Bus Developments to 1968

The first Preston Tramways Act was passed on 30th July 1900 and gave the Corporation the powers to construct seven principal sections of tramway to a gauge of 4ft 0ins. The powers in this Act provided for a tramway along Waterloo Road and Bray Street which would have formed a circular section around part of Ashton, had it ever been built. It also included a proviso for sections of track along Corporation Street and Moor Lane, neither of which were constructed. A second Act was passed on 23rd June 1902 and it was this Act that the Corporation followed for the construction of the town's electric tramway. A provision was also made to construct a line along Plungington Road. Under the Act the Corporation was required to widen several of the thoroughfares along which the lines were to be laid and this would not have been possible on Plungington Road so the line was never built. The 1902 Act stipulated that a gauge of 4ft 8½ins was to be used.

Table 1		
No.	**Length**	**Streets**
1900 Act		
1	2m 7f	Broadgate, Fishergate, Church Street, Stanley Street, New Hall Lane.
4	1m 3f	Lancaster Road, Ormskirk Road, North Road, Garstang Road.
8	1m 0f	Deepdale Road.
10	1m 1f	Harris Street, Friargate, Fylde Street, Fylde Road, Water Lane.
12	1m 3f	Water Lane, Tulketh Road, Long Lane, Waterloo Road*, Bray Street*.
15	0m 6f	Corporation Street*, Moor Lane*.
17	1m 4f	Mill Bank, Ribbleton Lane, Ribbleton Avenue.
1902 Act (additional)		
7	1m 1f	Watling Street Road.
20	1m 0f	Plungington Road*.

* Sections of line not constructed.
The omitted sections applied to short lengths of track for connections and passing loops.
Lengths are shown in miles and furlongs.

The first electric tram services commenced on 7th June 1904; one running from Lancaster Road via North Road, Garstang Road and Watling Street Road to Fulwood Barracks and another running via Church Street, Stanley Street and New Hall Lane to Farringdon Park. On the 30th June the service to Penwortham commenced with trams running through from the end of Broadgate to either Farringdon Park or the Withy Trees public house at Fulwood. By the following month trams were running in both directions as a circular route to Fulwood via either Deepdale Road or North Road. Also, from 9th July, a new electric tram service commenced running from Harris Street and then principally via Friargate, Fylde Road and Tulketh Road to Ashton with the terminus being situated at the junction of Long Lane (later part of Blackpool Road) and Waterloo Road. The electric tram network was completed with the opening of the route to the Bowling Green Hotel on Ribbleton Avenue on 26th January 1905. The route network then consisted of in excess of ten route miles.

All of Preston's new electric trams were built at the town's Strand Road Works which supplied trams, and later buses, to all corners of the globe. In 1904 the firm was known as the Electric Railway & Tramway Carriage Works. Thirty open-top double-deck cars were initially ordered to operate the new services. Nos. 1-26 were 4-wheel open-top double-deck cars powered by two 25hp motors, the standard tram of the era; whilst Nos. 27-30 were similar but larger capacity bogie cars driven by two 35hp motors. For the first eight years these cars maintained the services, although during that time all but three of the 4-wheel cars were fitted with top covers, allowing for an increase in capacity on the top deck of two. In 1912 three single-deck cars with enclosed saloons, Nos. 31-3, were obtained specifically to work the Ashton service. These were fitted with two 40hp motors and, although again built at Strand Road, the builder was then known as the United Electric Car Company. Although there were no extensions to the system a steady increase in traffic levels called for the acquisition of six new double-deck cars which were numbered 34-9. These had open balconies and were again fitted with two 40hp motors and provided seats for 52 passengers. In order to accommodate the additional trams new offices, fronting Deepdale Road with an extension to the car sheds, were opened in 1915.

In November 1919 it was decided that further trams were required and so six Dick, Kerr-built single-deck cars were bought from Sheffield Corporation. These cars were built at the beginning of the century and were originally open ended.

Before entering service they were mounted on new trucks which were acquired from the London County Council Tramways and soon after they were rebuilt in the Corporation's workshops with enclosed ends. Three similar cars, but built by Brush, followed in 1920. The Sheffield cars were numbered 40-8 but several were renumbered in 1932 to make way for the new TD2s, which were delivered in July of that year.

Despite initial proposals to open up further tram routes along Plungington Road and London Road, it was eventually decided to operate a service along the former using motorbuses. Consequently, three of Leyland's G7 models were purchased and these entered service on 23rd January 1922. They were dual-door buses with a total of 30 seats but the saloon was split into two sections. The livery worn was the same as that used on the trams at that time and the number sequence roughly followed on, with these three being given the numbers 51-3. A fourth similar vehicle, No. 54, entered service in June the following year. Further bus routes to Frenchwood and Ashton Lane Ends were started in June 1924 and for these five of the larger SG7s were purchased which were numbered 55-9. These had seating for 36 passengers, again in a partitioned saloon, although at least three of the batch were later modified inside and reduced to 32 seats. The engine was mounted alongside the driver, as opposed to in front of the driving position on the G7s. In March 1925, two of the smaller Leyland

A13s, Nos. 60/1, and a Leyland SG9, No. 62, all of which were bodied by English Electric, entered service.

In May 1925 a bus service commenced running from the Cemetery at Farringdon Park to Ashton Lane Ends via what was known as the Arterial Road (Blackpool Road). This had been made possible by the completion of a road bridge over the London North Western Railway line in December 1923. This new route ran on Sunday afternoons only and was principally a recreational route serving the Cemetery at one end and the nearby Haslam Park at the other. Up to this time all bus services had been in the hands of single-deckers. The first double-deck buses were introduced to the Lytham Road service in August 1926 when the Corporation purchased two Leyland Leviathans, Nos. 63/4, which had open back staircases and seating for 52 passengers. They were powered by an 8.0 litre petrol engine and ran on solid tyres. A third Leviathan No. 65, which was new the following year, had a smaller engine and seated seven fewer passengers. All three were fitted with pneumatic tyres in 1931.

Although route letters had been used on the tram routes from an early date these were actually later phased out in preference to just showing the destinations. However, by at least 1931 the bus routes were then being denoted by letters with PL in use for the Lytham Road service, 'A' for Ashton Lane Ends, FR for Frenchwood and HPC (Haslam Park – Cemetery) for the cross-town service.

The original tram depot buildings are seen soon after they were opened in 1904. The building to the left is the original office block which was demolished in 1915 to make way for the car shed extension and the new offices. Holmrook Road runs alongside the shed. No. 2 garage was built on the side of this building over the road. Some trams can just be seen inside and the photographer has caught the attention of some young children.

At least seven of the 1904 built 4-wheel cars can be seen inside the newly constructed car shed at Deepdale Road. Clearly visible are cars Nos. 17, 25, 15 and 23. For some reason the blind on No. 17 has been partially rolled out of the destination box. The enclosed area behind the two left hand roads is just discernible. The centre pillars were removed in 1936 and replaced by girders which spanned the full width of the structure. This shed, known as No. 1 garage, still formed part of the 21st century bus garage and the section on view was equipped as the docking shop in 1965.

A view inside the car sheds which were extended in 1915, almost certainly taken sometime in the last five months of 1934 after two of the tram tracks to the right had been removed to create more bus parking space. From left to right are one of the former Sheffield cars which had been renumbered to 12; former Lincoln English Electric car No. 13 with the other two, Nos. 18 and 22, behind; 1914 UEC Co car No. 36 and one of 1932 TD2s of the Nos. 41-50 batch. Visible through the side doorway is the rear of 1929 Leyland Lion No. 72 with another TD2, No. 49 and one of the 1934 lowbridge TD3cs alongside. The adjacent bus garage was only constructed in 1932. The front part of this garage continued to be used for parking buses until 1977 when it was converted into a purpose-built bodyshop with the docking shop in the section beyond the side entrance.

1912 United Electric Car Co built car No. 32 was one of three similar cars and is seen waiting on Fishergate Bridge outside the Central Railway Station for prospective match goers to Deepdale, sometime in the early 1930s. These cars were normally employed on the Ashton service.

In September 1928 the first in a long line of Leyland Titans entered service in the form of No. 66 which was an all-Leyland TD1. The body was of lowheight configuration and had seating for 48 passengers and was one of only five buses operated by the Corporation which had an open staircase. It is seen in a posed view between the Market Square and the Cenotaph in the town centre. Behind is the Court Sessions House and to the left of the building is the site of the Municipal Buildings (later known as the Town Hall) which were only opened in 1931. No. 66 passed to local operator Bamber Bridge Motor Services in March 1938 as their No. 1 and continued in use as a psv until 1946.

No. 53 was one of the first three motorbuses purchased by the Corporation in January 1922 and was a Leyland G7 with a 30-seat English Electric-built body. It is seen alongside the Town Hall in Cheapside on the Plungington Road service which was inaugurated on 23rd January. Note the 'Hackney Carriage' lettering above the registration plate.

In September 1929 four Leyland-bodied LT1s with 35-seat front entrance bodies entered the fleet and these were gainfully employed on the Frenchwood and Ashton services, including the cross-town service. No. 72 is seen inside No. 3 garage sometime in the early 1930s whilst No. 71 is seen in the same garage on 6th April 1939; the day after it had been involved in a serious accident which also involved lowbridge TD3c No. 4. Note that No. 71 has gained a somewhat ungainly route letter box. All four of the type were withdrawn in December 1939 and were used as emergency ambulance vehicles during the war.

Preston's first Leyland Titan was TD1 No. 66, which entered service in September 1928. This and No. 67, which was bought the following year, were the only two Titans with open back staircases. In each of the years 1928 and 1929 the Department, in conjunction with English Electric, embarked on the reconstruction of one of the single-deck trams. It is likely that former Sheffield cars Nos. 40 and 42 were used as the basis to construct the almost new double-deck cars, which were fully enclosed and had seating for 22 passengers in the lower saloon and leather cushioned seats with reversible backs for 40 passengers in the upper saloon. No. 42 was re-numbered to 30 in July 1932. Additionally, nine of the 1904 cars were rebuilt to a fully enclosed configuration during the mid-1920s (see chapter 6). The final trams to enter the Preston fleet were three English Electric-built low-height double-deck cars which were bought from Lincoln Corporation in July 1929. These cars were similar to Nos. 34-9 with regards to both their seating capacity and their open-ended balconies on the top deck and took the available numbers 13, 18 and 22. A batch of four Leyland-bodied LT1s, Nos. 71-4, entered service in September 1929 but they had fairly short lives with the undertaking, as all four were requisitioned for ambulance duties shortly after the start of WW2. This new generation of single-deckers was generally one of larger vehicles than those previously operated and they were painted in a different layout of maroon and cream with full lining out.

Two more English Electric-bodied TD1s, Nos. 51/2, entered service in October 1931 whilst, despite obtaining powers at this time to operate trolleybuses, the Transport Committee opted for more motorbuses to replace the ageing trams. Consequently, an order for 14 new buses was placed with the English Electric Co factory, comprising four more Leyland Lions, LT5s No. 75-8, and ten TD2s, Nos. 41-50. Whilst the Leyland-bodied Lions had their entrances at the front this latest batch of single-deck buses had a more traditional rear entrance and they also had three fewer seats. The TD2s were purchased to convert the Farringdon Park and Broadgate (Penwortham) services to motorbus operation which took place on 4th July 1932. Eleven trams were withdrawn as a consequence of this first conversion. In September a new weekday service commenced running from the Cemetery to Lane Ends (LEC) via a series of

back roads and was intended to provide a service to the mills in the Ashton district. Meanwhile, all but one of the first generation of single-deckers had been withdrawn by October 1933, with only No. 62 lingering on until April 1936. Three of the SG7s, Nos. 55/7/9, passed to Leyland Motors in March 1933, although what Leyland did with them is not recorded. Also in that year the Transport Department bought its first TIM ticket machines to replace the Bell Punch type and over a short period of time all the conductors were issued with them.

With the Transport Committee having set out their stall, the conversion of the remaining tram routes to motorbus operation quickly followed. The Ribbleton service substantially lost its trams in November 1933 and their replacements comprised four TD2s, Nos. 53, 68-70 and six TD3s, Nos. 54-9, all of which were bodied by English Electric. No. 53 was unusual in that the chassis was completed in October 1932 but it didn't receive its all-metal body until 12 months later. At the same time two more new single-deck buses entered the fleet; these were Lion LT5 No. 79 and Tiger TS4 No. 80, both of which were fitted with English Electric bodies which had seats for 32 passengers. Meanwhile, the last trams to Ribbleton are thought to have run in June 1934. It had long been the practice for routes to be linked across the town centre for operational purposes. The Penwortham 'P' (later Broadgate BR) service was linked with the Farringdon Park (FP) service and following the full conversion of the Ribbleton (R) service to motorbuses this service was linked with the PL. The latter service had been extended to Boys Lane in July 1933. On 6th August 1934 the Ashton (A) main route was converted to motorbus operation using ten lowbridge English Electric-bodied TD3cs, Nos. 1-10, which were necessary to pass under the height restricted Fylde Road Railway Bridge. No. 10, which was constructed with an all-metal body, didn't actually enter service until February 1935. At the same time another new route commenced running from Corporation Street to Ashton Lane Ends using the letter 'B' and which formed a complicated linked route with the Lane Ends 'A' route. It will be noted that at this time the letter 'A' was being used simultaneously for two different routes.

In 1932 an extension to garage the buses was constructed by local contractor, H H Topping of Fulwood, on the side of the tram car sheds over what had previously been Holmrook Road. A single tram line ran through the centre of the shed and out of the

One of a trio of 1940 highbridge TD5s, No. 38 passes the cemetery at the corner of Blackpool Road and New Hall Lane. It is likely the bus is heading back to the depot following a run on the cross-town service from Ashton Lane Ends as the destination is still showing Cemetery and the bus appears to be empty. No. 38 has been heavily rebuilt and now sports rubber-mounted flush windows.

1935 English Electric-bodied Leyland TD4 No. 26 is seen in Lune Street in the early 1950s. The Ashton A, Lane Ends C and Boys Lane/Queens Drive PL services were forced to circumnavigate the town centre following the introduction of a one-way traffic system in February 1939; an arrangement which continued until 1968 when the three services were rerouted via the adjacent Fox Street. Four years later a contra-flow bus lane was opened on Friargate which removed the services from the chronic traffic conditions around the Public Hall.

back entrance. The new bus garage included a side extension, which contained four inspection pits. These were later known as No. 2 and No. 3 garages. The following year the tram car shed was reduced to four parking roads. The two lines nearest to the adjoining bus garage were removed and the pit areas were concreted in to form additional capacity for garaging the buses. A side entrance from the bus garage to the newly built bus parking area in the tram shed was also constructed. This work was again carried out by Toppings. Following the cessation of tram operations, the remaining part of the tram car shed was converted to a bus parking area in 1936. This work was carried out by Thomas Blackburn & Sons and involved removing the steel stanchions supporting the roof and replacing them with steel girders which spanned the full width of the shed. Additionally, the tram lines and pits were removed and the floor re-concreted. At least two inspection pits, possibly four, were constructed at the top end of the garage. This was and still is known as No. 1 garage although in 2013 it housed the bodyshop and docking shop.

The final tramway replacement programme had involved the conversion of the Fulwood circular routes and was implemented in December 1935. At the time there were still 26 trams in use at the start of the year and only four more had been withdrawn as the final day approached. The last rites, on Sunday 15th December, were appropriately performed by car No. 24 which had also made the inaugural trip on 7th June 1904. In May the Corporation had placed a large order with Leyland and English Electric for 24 new buses; four TD4s, Nos. 11-14, and two LT7 Lions, Nos. 81/2, were fitted with all-metal Leyland-built bodies whilst a further 18 TD4s, Nos. 15-32, were bodied by English Electric. All were fitted with torque convertors and the splitting of the order for the construction of the bodywork was typical of the loyalty shown to both local firms. Virtually all of the trams were broken up at the depot by a Mr F Brown who purchased them for scrap for the princely sum of either £15 or £16 each.

Earlier in the year two former demonstration vehicles were acquired from Leyland Motors. These were Leyland lowbridge-bodied TD1 No. 60, which was originally new to Birmingham City Transport in August 1928 and with whom it had carried a Short-built body for just nine months in 1929, and Leyland all-metal-bodied TD3c No. 61. Work was carried out on both vehicles by the Corporation at

a total cost of £190 before they entered service. A further 13 Titans were put into service between September 1936 and March 1940; these included three more TD4s, Nos. 62-4, and eight TD5s, Nos. 33-40, which were nominally required for route expansions to Ashton Lane Ends (C), Holme Slack (HS) and Moorside (M) [Moor Nook]. The other two were lowbridge TD5c No. 4, which was a direct replacement for TD3c CK 4904 which was written off in an accident in April 1939, and No. 65, the chassis of which was built by Leyland as a prototype TD6 in January 1939. However, it was modified as a TD7 before being fitted with a Leyland-built body and it entered service with the Corporation in March 1940. In April 1937 a new single-deck bus service had commenced running to Fulwood Row (GL) via St Paul's Road, St Thomas' Road, Deepdale Road and Watling Street Road. The following May a handful of journeys were extended deeper in to the countryside to terminate at Long Sand Lane (it was only from 1957 that the letters LS were used for these journeys). To complete the pre-war bus fleet a final English Electric-bodied Lion LT7c, No. 83, was part of the December 1937 intake.

Apart from Nos. 50/3 and 70, all the TD1s and TD2s were originally powered by petrol engines but all of the TD2s later received oil (diesel) engines (see chapter 6). The last petrol-engined bus in service was TD1 No. 51, which was withdrawn in May 1947. Most of the later TDs were fitted with torque converters and a programme of fitting gear boxes was started in October 1943. The full programme was never completed and Nos. 2, 5, 10, 30/1 and 61 were all withdrawn without being converted. Similarly, all but the last four single-deckers were originally powered by petrol engines, but Nos. 75-9 were also fitted with oil engines in 1937. Also Nos. 76/9, 80 had their standard seating removed in January 1942 to be replaced by perimeter seating for 28 passengers but at the same time the standing room was increased. Whilst Nos. 76/9 were never altered back, No. 80 reverted back to its original layout in October 1945, when it was considerably rebuilt by Lancashire Aircraft at Samlesbury.

During WW2 the Transport Department had to make do and mend. Although no new buses were received after March 1940, nine TD2s were re-bodied by English Electric at Strand Road, with their new bodies seating exactly the same number as the old ones. Various strategic measures were implemented during the war, one of which included the dispersal of the fleet as a precautionary measure in the event of an enemy attack on the depot. No. 1 garage was taken over by the English Electric Company in October 1940 to assist in the war effort. Consequently, arrangements were made to park some buses in the grounds of the old Gas Works off Moor Lane. The following year an additional arrangement was made to park some buses on spare ground behind the Deepdale Modern School. In line with other fleets throughout the country the headlights were dimmed and the fronts of the mud-guards were painted white. As an added measure the conductors were issued with torches and gas detectors were fitted to some buses. Services were amended to save fuel, both by cutting back on sections of route and reducing the number of timetabled departures and the number of stops served. Several TD2s were loaned to both the London Passenger Transport Board and Lancashire United Transport (see Table 2).

Table 2			
Buses loaned to LPTB		Buses loaned to LUT	
No.	Dates	No.	Dates
42*	31/10/40 – 23/7/41	42	-/8/41 – 20/7/43
48	25/10/40 - -/7/41	48	/8/41 – 1/2/44
49	31/10/40 - -/7/41	50	-/8/41 - -12/41
50*	25/10/40 – 23/7/41	68	-/9/41 - -/12/41
68	-/10/40 - -/7/41		
70	-/10/40 - -/7/41		
* Nos. 42 and 50 were based at Nunhead garage for route 12. LPTB buses were fitted with a plaque inside inscribed 'London 1940-41'.			

In the last few months of the war four TD3s were re-bodied by Crofts of Glasgow, one of which was lowbridge No. 9. On cessation of hostilities orders were placed for several of the new post-war Leylands, the PD1 and its variant the PD1A. Originally these were to have been 8ft wide buses but the specification was changed to 7ft 6ins, due to delivery delays and route restrictions which would have precluded the use of wider buses on certain routes. Thirty-one of the type entered service between July 1946 and October 1947, all with bodywork designed by Leyland. Some were constructed by nearby Samlesbury Engineering whilst others were built at Walter Alexander's factory in Falkirk. Eight, Nos. 60/6/7, 103-7, were of a lowbridge construction with a sunken gangway on the offside of the top deck, for use on the Ashton A service. Initially the PD1s were used to increase service levels with only two TD's, Nos. 50/1, being correspondingly withdrawn.

Alterations to the Lane Ends services were implemented on 11th November 1946 when service 'A' was re-lettered to 'B' running to Inkerman Street and the previous service lettered 'B' became the 'D' which was then linked with the 'C' which had latterly been linked with the Holme Slack. This arrangement was short lived however as from April 1947 the 'D' was then linked with the Frenchwood (FR) service and buses on the Ashton 'C' reverted to running through to Holme Slack. In May a new single-deck operated service which used the route letters TS commenced running from Harris Street via Fishergate, Lune Street, Friargate and Moor Lane before working its way through Plungington to terminate in Trafford Street. This remains the only stage service to have ever been routed along Moor Lane. The TS was short lived and only just survived to the end of the year being withdrawn on 31st December.

Discussions had taken place with Ribble Motor Services and Scout Motor Services concerning the introduction of a number of jointly operated services which were to serve adjoining areas just outside the town boundary. Consequently, on 1st January 1948 a significant number of changes were made to the route network. The FR/D linked service became the P1 and was extended beyond Ashton Lane Ends to Victoria Park Drive at Lea. New services P2 and P4 commenced running from Lightfoot Lane in Fulwood to either the Plough Inn or Crookings Lane at Penwortham and the P5 started from the Anchor Inn at Hutton and ran through to Ribbleton Gamull Lane. The Ribbleton Chatburn Road 'R' service was extended to Gamull Lane as the GL and the GL and P5 operated to a co-ordinated timetable from the town centre to Ribbleton. In consequence of the extended Ribbleton service taking the letters GL, the Fulwood Row service henceforth displayed the letters FR which had previously been used by the Frenchwood service. The Crookings Lane service was short lived and from May all journeys ran as the P2. By the end of the year operation of the P2 had become the preserve of Ribble whilst the P5 was exclusively worked by Corporation buses. Ribble provided just one vehicle for the P1.

By October 1949 a number of pre-war Titans had been laid up. These were advertised for sale, but without their engines and gearboxes which were removed beforehand. The buses concerned were Nos. 5, 31, 57/9 and 61, all of which were bought by local dealers. During their years in service with

Number. 65 was a Leyland-bodied TD7 and was the last pre-war bus to enter the fleet in March 1940. It is seen outside the Territorial Army barracks in Deepdale Road in the mid-1950s on football special duty, by which time its appearance had been somewhat altered with, amongst other modifications, the acquisition of a single destination screen and flush-mounted windows with rubber surrounds.

Number 14 was one of four Leyland TD4cs with an all-metal H30/24R Leyland constructed body, which was part of a larger order of buses which was received in November and December 1935 to replace the last of the Corporation's trams. It lasted in service until June 1955. Many of Leyland's official photographs were taken in the town's Worden Park.

The original Ashton Lane Ends routes were peculiar in that they started from Corporation Street, near the Railway Station. By the early 1950s only the Ashton B service ran from this location. 1937 Leyland LT7 No. 83 waits to depart for Lane Ends via Maudland Bank, Pedder Street, Waterloo Road, Long Lane, Lytham Road and Inkerman Street. No. 83 was withdrawn in 1953 and the Ashton 'B' was converted to double-deck operation in March 1954. The starting point was moved to the town centre a couple of months later and the route survived until February 1965, latterly being the preserve of PD1s. The buildings in the background were still in use in 2013.

Number. 61 was the last of a batch of 10 Leyland-bodied PD2/10s, comprising eight highbridge and two lowbridge types, which entered service in May 1954. It is seen parked in St Thomas' Road on Football Special duty when probably only a year or two old. It was withdrawn in December 1963 and was the penultimate PD3/6 rebuild in a protracted programme which spanned some eight years. Note the temporary bus stands with the destinations painted on. The Lime Kiln was a pub at the junction of Aqueduct Street and Stocks Road where some buses started from to take supporters to the match; the building still exists as a Chinese restaurant.

In November 1955 a batch of five Leyland PD2/10s with MCW Orion-built bodies entered service with the undertaking. No. 82 is seen outside the Parish Church in Church Street in the early 1960s and still has its distinctive rear chrome bumpers. These buses gave exceptional service and were not withdrawn until 1976 when all but No. 79 were sold to G Jones at Carlton for scrap. For many years buses worked through from Farringdon Park to either Boys Lane or Queens Drive on an alternate basis with the combined service running at five minute intervals at the busiest times.

Crossley-bodied Leyland PD2/10 No. 24 was the first of 18 of the type to be delivered on 29th June 1956. It is seen posed on Preston North End's Deepdale car park before entering service two days later. No. 24 had a reasonably long life with the undertaking and was not withdrawn until July 1975 but unfortunately it ended its days in the Barnsley scrap yard of G Jones. No. 31 of the same type was the only former Preston PD2 to be saved for preservation.

the undertaking several alterations were made to various PD1s and a small number of TDs, such as the removal of the body side mouldings and the replacement of the separate destination and route letter screens with a single screen; whilst some also gained flush mounted windows on overhaul. The pre-war livery of maroon with three cream bands was continued after the war, except the buses were no longer lined out. Over the next decade the livery layout was changed several times and all of the PD1s are thought to have finished their service in maroon with a single cream band. It was in 1950 that the TIM type ticket machines started to be replaced by the Ultimate machine.

Following the early post-war influx of PD1s there was a three year gap (excepting the arrival of the 2 PS1s) before the next new buses entered service, at the end of 1950, in the form of 20 PD2/1s, Nos. 108-27. These were responsible for the demise of a similar number of pre-war Titans and wore a new livery application which included cream window surrounds and was radically different to the maroon and three cream bands layout. Some of the PD2/1s amassed over 20 years of service and Nos. 122-6 survived long enough to be painted in the later adopted blue and ivory livery. Continuing the pre-war bus replacement programme, two batches of Leyland-bodied PD2/10s were ordered for delivery in 1952 and 1954 and each consisted of eight highbridge and two lowbridge buses. These introduced a further livery modification in that the cream was omitted from the upper window surrounds. An additional feature, which was fitted to these buses, was a rear chrome bumper. The numbers applied to the second batch were somewhat haphazard as they missed out certain numbers still carried by some of the surviving TD3s and PD1s. Not long afterwards Leyland Motors ceased building bus bodies for the home market, and consequently the remaining PD2/10s were bodied by other manufacturers. The last remaining pre-war single-deckers, Nos. 80-2, were taken out of service in March 1954 and, along with the already withdrawn Nos. 79 and 83, they passed to AMCC, a dealer based in Stratford, East London.

In the post war recovery period of the early 1950s several more new services were commenced to newly constructed housing estates at Brookfield (CR), Moor Nook (M) and Larches (P1). The Brookfield service ran via Cromwell Road whilst the service to Moor Nook took the letter 'M' with the former Moorside service adopting the letters

MN. The service to Larches was a deviation of the service to Lea which was extended to Aldfield Avenue with buses serving each destination alternately. At the end of December 1956 both the Sunday LEC service and the Saturdays only Moor Nook service (M) were withdrawn. The weekday cross-town Works service consequently adopted the letters LEC in lieu of HPC.

Five more Leyland PD2/10s, Nos. 79-83, entered service in November 1955 and these were bodied by MCW at their Birmingham factory. Another eighteen of the chassis type had been ordered for delivery in 1956/7, with the order for the bodies having been placed with Park Royal. They were in fact assembled at their subsidiary works, the former Crossley factory in Stockport. The Crossleys were a protracted order spanning some 18 months and they also introduced yet another livery variation with only a single cream band between decks. The last PD2 to enter service was No. 31, in December 1957. Coincidentally, this bus was also one of the last two PD2s in service and is the only Preston bus of its type to survive into preservation. Both the MCWs and the Crossleys were also fitted with the rear bumpers.

The last TDs in service were Nos. 38-40 and 65, all of which were withdrawn at the end of December 1958, when the first batch of PD3s entered service. Many of the TDs were bought for further use. Nos. 1, 4 (RN 8887) and 56 passed to Paramount Coachways in Skeffington Road, whilst Nos. 19 and 35 were used by Leylux of Chorley as Mobile Showrooms. London dealers took Nos. 3, 8, 21, 60 and 66 whilst No. 62 was converted by a local farmer into a cattle transporter. W North of Leeds acquired 21 vehicles in total, many of which saw no further use.

Modifications to the PD2/10s included removing the chrome bumpers and increasing their seating capacity which was done in a rolling programme between 1958 and 1962. Several of the Crossleys, and all of the MCWs, had their separate destination and route letter screens replaced by a single screen. In September 1966 four buses were used for livery experiments, with Nos. 33/5, 43 and 81 all being painted in different arrangements and shades of blue and white or ivory. The scheme of mid-blue and ivory used on No. 35 was ultimately adopted as the new fleet livery. Of the PD2/10s, only Nos. 25-8 and 30 did not receive the new colours. Sadly, virtually all the PD2s were sold to scrap dealers

Leyland PD2/1 No. 118 entered service in January 1951. In this June 1969 view it is seen dropping off workers in Friargate on a Saturday lunchtime Works Special from Strand Road. No. 118 was withdrawn in April 1970 and was sold to Geoff Lister of Bolton.

Leyland lowbridge-bodied PD1 No. 67 was one of three similar vehicles received in December 1946 for use on the Ashton Pedders Lane service which passed under Fylde Road Railway Bridge. It is seen parked close to the Transport Offices in Lancaster Road in the mid-1950s. It still retains the mouldings below the upper deck windows which originally defined the position of the top cream band. Withdrawn in June 1958 No. 67 was sold to Barton Transport the following February with whom it saw service for another four or more years.

1958 MCW-bodied Leyland PD3/5 No. 65 is seen crossing the junction of Ribbleton Avenue and Blackpool Road with an inbound journey from Ribbleton in the early 1960s. No. 65 was withdrawn in November 1977 only to be reinstated the following month and it then continued in service until May 1979. It was then sold to Geoff Lister of Bolton and continued to be used in various guises until at least the end of the millennium. This junction remains largely unaltered today although the traffic signal pole is somewhat of a museum piece compared with 21st century installations.

This interesting early 1960s view shows 1949 Leyland PS1 No. 74 and 1959 PD3/6 Rebuild No. 9 passing the open covered market in Lancaster Road. The two buses are on some sort of special working which has originated from the Town Hall further up the road. Many a young teenager (the author included) would have bought their first vinyl 45 from Brady's record shop which later relocated to Crystal House. No. 74 was withdrawn in December 1968 and was later converted for use as a Mobile Polling Station, which duty it performed for most of the 1970s. Along with its classmate, No. 75, it is now preserved.

Seen in a deserted town centre (probably on a Sunday as the Harris Library gates are closed) is 1961 MCW-bodied Leyland PD3/4 No. 18 on the Gamull Lane stand in Jacson Street. It is working the jointly operated P5 service from Hutton to Ribbleton. No. 18 was the second of the batch to be withdrawn in August 1977 and was sold to one of the Barnsley breakers for scrap the following May. Apart from No. 16, which was withdrawn a few months earlier in February for conversion to a Recovery Vehicle, the remaining five lasted until early 1980 when they were replaced by the second batch of Alexander-bodied Atlanteans, Nos. 141-50.

1962 Leyland/PCTD PD3/6 Rebuild No. 50 stands alongside the Harris Library & Museum in Harris Street. This bus was repainted blue and ivory in August 1967 whilst the Brookfield services were amongst the first converted to 'PAYB' operation the following December. Behind the bus can be seen the Ribble Booking and Enquiry Offices in Lancaster Road.

following their withdrawal by the undertaking, with all but Nos. 31, 54/7, 79 and 110/6/9 ending up in various Barnsley breakers' yards. MCW-bodied No. 79 was sold to Jeff Brownhut, in May 1976, and was painted to advertise various Promotions; the first of which was on the town's Moor Park. No. 116 passed from Geoff Lister at Bolton to the Ingleton Caving Club and is reported to have ended its days in Turkey.

The Brookfield services were re-organised in July 1958 when a new service commenced running via Deepdale Road using the letters BF and which terminated at a newly constructed turning circle at the junction of Watling Street Road and Croasdale Avenue. At the same time the CR was cut back from Fulwood Row to turn at the same location. Seven more PD2s had been ordered for delivery during the course of the year and it was intended to fit the chassis with the 'Beverley Bar' style of double deck body, in order that they could be used on the Ashton A service under Fylde Road Railway Bridge. However, in 1957, the road surface under the bridge was lowered thus removing the restriction on the type of buses which could pass underneath. Consequently, the order was changed to one of seven PD3/5s, which were bodied by MCW. Tenders for the bodywork had also been submitted by Massey, Park Royal, Burlingham, Longwell Green, East Lancs and Willowbrook. Indeed MCW was not the lowest tenderer but was the preferred bidder. The PD3/5s had pneumocyclic gears, although No. 67 was later fitted with a synchromesh gearbox, which was also fitted to the second batch of new PD3s. Nos. 62-8 entered service in January 1959 and their larger size must have taken some getting used to, compared with the PD1s and PD2s. Indeed, in the first few weeks of operation, Nos. 64/5 were involved in accidents which required costly repairs. The next PD3 to enter service was actually Rebuild No. 9, in November 1959. This was followed by Nos. 5 and 2 in July 1960 and 1961 respectively. Whereas No. 9 had 41 seats on the upper deck all subsequent Rebuilds had 38. The last rebuilt lowbridge PD2, No. 10, entered service as a PD3 in February 1962 (see chapter 6).

The Transport Committee had deliberated on what type of vehicle should be ordered next and had proposed to order five 78-seat Atlanteans for the next batch of new buses. Consequently, in March 1960, MCW-bodied Leyland Atlantean demonstrator, 398 JTB, was trialled on the Gamull

Lane service. However, the Committee eventually opted to purchase a further seven MCW-bodied PD3s, Nos. 13-9, for their 1961 intake, which were received in August. Highbridge examples, Nos. 50/1, were the next two Rebuild PD3s to come out of the bodyshop, before another batch of new vehicles was taken into stock. Nos. 84-90 were a batch of PD3A/1s, again with MCW bodywork but with the so called 'St Helens' style of front, as opposed to having an exposed radiator. These entered service in November 1963 and were followed by a further batch of five similar buses in March 1965, which were numbered 69-73. Finally, two further Rebuilds were completed in April 1965 (61) and September 1967 (59). All the PD3s, except No. 59, carried three liveries during their time with the undertaking. Whereas No. 59 was turned out in blue and ivory, all the rest originally wore the maroon and cream colours. From November 1973 they were progressively repainted into the mainly ivory with blue relief layout. Only No. 88 ever carried an advert livery when it was sponsored by Dorman Smith for the 1972 Preston Guild.

The first two PD1s to be withdrawn were lowbridge buses, Nos. 105/7, in January 1959. Thereafter, more of the type were withdrawn each year through to 1965. Nos. 72/3, 85/6 and 98 were all converted for use as mobile Polling Stations, in August 1964. The most spectacular incident to befall one of the type occurred on 18th March 1960 when No. 6(106) took a wrong turning at the bottom of Waterloo Road and ended up wedged under the infamous 'Danger Bridge' which carried the Preston to Blackpool railway line. It was deemed uneconomical to repair and was eventually converted for use as a recovery vehicle. In October 1961 several of the type were sold to W North's of Leeds and Nos. 52, 71, 88/9, 90/9 and 102 were immediately purchased by Samuel Ledgard, who ran them for a further six years on local services from Armley. Also, lowbridge models Nos. 66/7 and 105 saw further service with Barton Transport. No. 88 eventually found its way into preservation as a long term restoration project.

A new extension to the bus garage was opened in April 1964 to the rear of Nos. 1 & 2 garages, providing a considerable amount of additional covered accommodation for the buses. The construction work was carried out by Connolly Brothers Ltd of Rawtenstall and included a piped heating system. The following year a new Docking

1963 MCW-bodied Leyland PD3A/1 No. 87 waits alongside Miller Arcade whilst 1958 MCW-bodied Leyland PD3/5 No. 62 waits on the FP stand, outside Crystal House, circa 1968. The blue and ivory livery was only introduced from the beginning of 1967 and No. 87 was repainted in November of that year. The MN service used this stand from December 1960 until the new Bus Station was opened in October 1969.

In October 1969 the new Central Bus Station was opened and this replaced the Bus Stations at Starchhouse Square, Fox Street and Tithebarn Street. Viking Motors 1949 Daimler CVD6 No. 4, with a lowbridge Strachan body, waits to depart Starchhouse Square Bus Station around 1951. Behind can be seen buses belonging to Scout Motor Services and Bamber Bridge Motor Services. Viking was absorbed by Ribble Motors in November 1952.

Shop was established in part of No. 1 garage. The writing had been on the wall for sometime for the Ashton 'B' and it was finally withdrawn after service on 12th February 1965. To fill the gap on Waterloo Road the Lea journeys on the P1 were re-routed via Water Lane, Bray Street and Waterloo Road and at the same time were re-numbered to P3. That same weekend, another jointly operated service, numbered P4, commenced running from the Express Coach Station to serve a new housing development at Ingol, to the north of the town.

In August 1966 a Leyland Panther had been taken on loan from Kingston-upon-Hull City Transport for evaluation purposes and the following month members of the Transport Committee visited the Burnley Colne & Nelson undertaking to inspect that operator's 'One Person Operated' buses. An order had been placed with MCW to provide the bodies for another five Leyland PD3s but this was cancelled following these two events. A Panther Cub demonstrator, YTB 771D, with a Strachan B43D body was also taken on loan from Leyland Motors for a trial period in April 1967. The minds of the Committee had finally been made up but as the undertaking prepared to enter a period of standardisation with a plethora of 'Pay-as-you-Board' (PAYB) equipped buses, a virtually all Leyland Titan fleet still maintained the services. At the end of November 1968 the fleet size stood at 95 vehicles (not dissimilar to the 102 vehicles operated in December 2013) consisting of 4 PD1s, 55 PD2s, 34 PD3s and 2 PS1s.

Crossley-bodied PD2/10 No. 20 entered service in April 1957 and is seen pulling away from the David Jones Men's Outfitters Bus Stop at the bottom of Tulketh Brow, closely pursued by Ribble lowbridge Atlantean No. 1804 which is on service 180 to Cleveleys. Whilst this view dates from the early 1960s, before the Lea journeys were renumbered to P3, No. 20 lasted in service until May 1975.

Leyland PD1 No. 84 has a Leyland designed body but was constructed at Walter Alexander's factory in Falkirk and entered service in July 1946. It was one of several Titans which were modified with a one piece destination screen. In this early 1960s view it is seen outside the Harris Library in Birley Street, alongside one of the characteristic town centre bus shelters.

MCW-bodied Leyland Panther No. 205 was one of a batch of five, which, along with Marshall-bodied Nos. 206-15, entered service on the first 'PAYB' services on 2nd December 1968. Only the MCW batch had the blue waist band and front panel. This view shows No. 205 passing the distinctive Stephenson Terrace in Deepdale Road, circa 1969.

2. Fleet Standardisation

There was a significant gap between the entry into service of the last conventional double-deckers, in April 1965, and the next generation of buses which appeared in the form of 15 Leyland Panthers, which dispensed with the conductor and introduced the concept of 'Pay-As-You-Board' (PAYB) operation to the unsuspecting travelling public of Preston. It had taken many months of negotiation to reach an agreement with the unions to operate these vehicles. Eventually the Corporation received its first Panther, No. 201, from MCW in June 1968 but initially it was used for driver familiarisation. These were the first buses purchased for one person operation and comprised MCW-bodied Nos. 201-5 and Marshall-bodied Nos. 206-15. Both batches were dual-door buses with seating for 47 passengers and were powered by a Leyland 0.600 engine. As became the practice over many years one of the new buses, No. 209, was displayed on the Market Square between 18th & 25th November, for the travelling public to inspect.

The first route conversions took place on Monday 2nd December 1968 when the Brookfield (BF, CR, FR, LS), Broadgate (BR) and Fulwood circular (D, F) services were all converted to operation with Leyland Panthers. The longer buses must have taken some getting used to, however, as a number of the type were involved in accidents and Nos. 202/5/9/11/3 all received significant damage in the first three months of operation. However, No. 214 was probably the most unluckiest vehicle, as it was badly damaged on 29th May 1970 when it was in collision with Crossley-bodied PD2 No. 20 on the Bus Station and only a few months later it received further damage when it hit a lamp standard at the bottom of Grimshaw Street; if that was not enough bad luck, some ten years later it was in collision with Ribble Leyland National No. 388. The jointly operated P1/P3 services were the next routes to be converted in April 1970; the Moor Nook followed in December 1971 with the Ashton services to Lane Ends and Pedders Lane following a year later, although these three services remained crew operated on Sundays using PD3s, until September 1976. During this tranche of conversions the new Bus Station had been opened on Sunday 12th October 1969 with all services being transferred from their town centre street stands. This resulted in the closure of the town's other Bus Stations at Starchhouse Square, Fox Street and Tithebarn Street which were all eventually swept away by redevelopment. To facilitate the subsequent route conversions a further seven Panthers, numbered 216-22 and again bodied by Marshalls of Cambridge, entered service between February and April 1970. These were followed by two batches of Seddon Pennine-bodied machines, Nos. 223-9 and Nos. 230-6, and five third hand acquisitions, AUE 309-13J from Midland Red. The latter had been new to Stratford Blue Motor Services but passed, with that operator, to Midland Red who promptly disposed of them. At first they were given the fleet numbers 230-4 but these were changed to 237-41 to make way for the last batch of new Panthers. The former Midland Red machines were used in 'as acquired condition' for some nine years before being modified to receive six additional seats and new exit doors.

The Panthers replaced an equal number of older buses over a four year period. First to go, in December 1968, were the two Tigers Nos. 74/5, both of which still survive as preserved vehicles. Also of significance was the withdrawal of the last five PD1s, Nos. 91-4/7, at the same time. Inroads were also made into the PD2 fleet; Crossley-bodied Nos. 25-8, 30/5/7 and the complete batch of 1952 highbridge bodied Leylands, Nos. 41-8, were all withdrawn, whilst the last three PD2/1s, Nos. 123/4/6, were retired in 1972. Five of the Crossleys were the last buses to run in the maroon livery, whilst the other two had been used as driver training vehicles. All of the Titans were sold for scrap to various merchants in the Barnsley area.

Marshall-bodied Panther, No. 207, spent some 21 months off the road prior to July 1978, laid up with mechanical problems. Of the second batch of Seddon-bodied machines, No. 236 was used as a test bed for CAV Transmission and did not enter service with the undertaking until April 1973, although it was seen in the Guild Trades procession in September 1972; it also carried a promotional livery for the Red Rose Rambler Ticket. All but ten of the type were rebuilt at the back to a modified layout, in 1978/9, to provide easier access to the cooling system filler tank which was at the rear of the bus. The last Panthers had entered service in August 1972 and no new buses were received in 1973. All of the Panthers were retrospectively fitted with fareboxes and this type of fare collection was first introduced to the Fulwood circular routes from

Marshall-bodied Leyland Panther No. 207 was one of the first fifteen 'PAYB' buses to enter service in December 1968 and is seen on the Broadgate stand at the top of Fishergate. At the time the Brookfield (BF, CR, FR and LS) and Broadgate (BR) services were linked for operational purposes. The other routes converted at the same time were the Fulwood circulars, 'F' and 'D'. The film showing at the cinema was a low budget spaghetti western first released in 1968.

Seen in a guise in which it never operated is Marshall Camair-bodied Leyland Panther XNX 135H which initially became No. 234 when it joined the Preston fleet in November 1971. It was renumbered to 241 the following May. These five buses were ordered by Stratford Blue but passed to Midland Red along with the former operator. Whilst with Midland Red they were re-registered to AUE 309-13J but were not used by that operator either. Although somewhat unconventional compared with the other Panthers in the fleet they remained in service until June 1983 when they were replaced by the last batch of new Atlanteans. Note the large luggage pen to the left of the centre doors which was not removed until 1980 when the seating capacity was increased by six to B47D.

1963 MCW-bodied Leyland PD3A/1 No. 88 carried this special colour scheme for the 1972 Guild from April to September. Seen departing the Bus Station for Pedders Lane this view was either taken on a Sunday as the 'A' was converted to 'PAYB' operation on Mon-Sat from 6th May 1971 or it was standing in for a Panther.

Number 5 was the second of the lowbridge PD2 conversions to the PD3/6 configuration and entered service as such in July 1960. It was the first bus painted in the reverse ivory and blue livery in November 1973. The Holme Slack service began operation on 17th February 1936 and for many years it was linked across town with the Lane Ends C. In May 1987 a parallel mini-bus service, numbered 114, was introduced which ran beyond Holme Slack to Fairfax Road. The 14, as such, ran to Holme Slack for the last time in October 1997 being completely replaced by the 114 which then assumed the number 14. From June 2010 the service was extended to Brookfield following the withdrawal of service 7. No.5 is seen leaving the Holme Slack terminus on 24th May 1977. It initially passed to Brown & Root following its withdrawal in December 1978 and after exchanging owners several times it was used as a donor in the restoration of sister vehicle No.2 in 1996.

1st October 1973. Earlier that year, in May, Boys Lane ceased to be used as a terminus by buses on the PL service with all journeys extended through to Queens Drive. In November a second joint service to Ingol was started which was numbered P6 and although it was initially routed via Ashton Lane Ends, the route was radically altered two years later to run via Garstang Road, Lytham Road and Cadley Causeway. Only a handful of journeys were provided on Monday to Friday and it was crew operated until 1980.

Three demonstration vehicles were trialled between April and August 1972, comprising Alexander-bodied Atlantean, XKC 831K, from Merseyside PTE and Leyland Nationals, DAO 251K and FRM 499K, from Leyland Motors. Significantly, all three buses had dual-door bodywork. Government grants eventually became available towards the cost of purchasing 'PAYB' equipped double-deckers and, following the trials, the Transport Committee approved the purchase of ten Atlanteans the following March. They had 82-seat dual-door bodies built by Alexander and were numbered 101-10. The first two were delivered in December 1974 and they were painted in the revised ivory and blue double-deck livery, which was first applied to PD3/6 No. 5 in November 1973. No. 102 had the distinction of being the first of the type to enter service on 3rd January 1975. As 'PAYB' vehicles, they were initially tried on the Fulwood circulars, the D and F, but they were also used with conductors and tended to turn up on various services. In April of the following year they were fitted with speakers on the top deck for an audio advertising contract. All the buses replaced were Crossley-bodied PD2/10s, leaving just Nos. 29, 31/4 of the type still in service at the end of 1975.

In October 1974, what was to be the final joint service commenced running to the Savick estate and was again routed via Ashton Lane Ends. Another crewed route, PD2s were frequent performers until the Bristol LHS mini-buses took over on 30th August 1976. With the introduction of these three new buses further estate routes commenced at the same time running to Callon (CL) and Grange (G). The latter was routed via Ribbleton Lane and the Moor Nook estate before being radically altered in January 1978 to run via New Hall Lane, whilst the former ran for the last time on 1st July 1977. The Bristols were numbered 242-4 and were the first bus chassis ever bought from outside of the Leyland stable. No. 242 was fitted out with high backed seats

with the intention of using it on Private Hire work. To this end it was fitted with a boot and luggage lockers in 1982. They were not ideally suited to intensive bus work as the Duple bodies were fitted with narrow doorways and steep stepped entrances, which made entering and alighting difficult for some passengers. During their service with Preston they were subjected to two re-numberings, finally ending up as Nos. 42-4.

Four more batches of Atlanteans were ordered, to be delivered year on year between 1976 and 1980. The first thirty were bodied by East Lancashire Coachbuilders and were built in three batches of ten. Nos. 111-20 were received in September and November 1976 and replaced the last ten PD2s; the last of which, Nos. 31 and 83, ran on the Farringdon Park service on Thursday 7th October. Also of some significance was the withdrawal of the first PD3, No. 66, in December as a result of mechanical failure. The next ten Atlanteans, Nos. 121-30, were received between October 1977 and January 1978, and were a somewhat protracted delivery. Consequently, more PD3s fell by the wayside and MCW-bodied examples, Nos. 16/8 and 63/7/8 were all retired during 1977, along with three of the Rebuilds, Nos. 9, 10 and 51. That year also saw the last significant alteration made to the depot when the remainder of No. 1 garage was converted for use as a new bodyshop.

A solitary example of the next batch of Atlanteans, No. 134, was delivered on 16th December 1978 but was initially used as a demonstration vehicle. It was to be April 1979 before it entered regular service with the undertaking. The remainder of the batch, Nos. 131-3/5-40, were received between March and June, with the last entering service on 3rd July. Throughout 1978 and 1979 another 13 PD3s were withdrawn, which included the remaining five Rebuilds. At the end of May a Dennis Dominator was taken on loan from East Staffordshire District Council and was used as a crewed vehicle on the GL and PL services and as a 'PAYB' vehicle on the Fulwood circulars. Numbered 29 in the ESDC fleet it stayed with the undertaking for five weeks, whilst at the same time Atlantean No. 115 was loaned to East Staffordshire in return. At the same time Leyland Titan, BCK 706R, was trialled as a crewed vehicle on services FP and HS.

The Transport Committee had approached Alexanders for the supply of bodywork for some of the aforementioned vehicles, but the firm had

Number. 53 was one of eight highbridge Leyland-bodied PD2/10s which entered service in March 1954. Whilst Nos. 50/1/9 and 61 were all rebuilt as PD3/6s the remaining four, Nos. 49, 53/4/7 continued in service until the end of 1975. Nos. 54/7 were then converted to permanent driver tuition vehicles but No. 53 was not so lucky and the bus was sold to G Jones at Carlton for scrap. This view is taken in Edgar Street at the back of the Bus Station and must have been the result of a diversionary route being in operation indicating that the main exit must have been closed.

Fourteen years before actually operating their own Leyland Nationals two of the type were trialled in July and August 1972. FRM 499K was on loan from Leyland Motors and is seen in Tulketh Road, Ashton heading for the Pedders Lane terminus. An Atlantean was also tried at the same time and it was this latter type of vehicle which the Transport Committee later decided would be the bus for the future.

During the 1972 Guild week, several routes from the north and west of the town terminated at St Peters Square, off Fylde Road. Virtually brand new Seddon-bodied Leyland Panther No. 231 and MCW-bodied Leyland PD2/10s Nos. 79 and 81 can be clearly seen in this view with PD3/6 Rebuild No. 5 and another Seddon Panther bringing up the rear. The attractive chrome beading was replaced in later life by simple painted metal strips. This area is now the focal point of the University of Central Lancashire (UCLAN). The trees on the left and the tower blocks of flats have since been removed from this view although the houses were still occupied in 2013.

The Ingol estate was built in the early to mid 1960s and gained its first bus service on 13th February 1965 when a handful of journeys were provided to serve Cottam Avenue/Barry Avenue with the then newly introduced jointly operated P4. 1975 Alexander-bodied Leyland Atlantean No. 106 is seen in Barry Avenue on the estate in March 1981 on what at the time was the Sundays and evenings only variant of the 34 service but which was alternatively routed via Brook Street, vice Fylde Road. Service 44 still covered more or less the same roads in 2013 although it was then in the hands of Optare Solos. No. 106 was withdrawn in July 1987 and was one of six of the batch which were sold to the North Western Road Car Company.

Although the Savick estate was a product of the early 1960s house building programme it didn't gain its first bus route until 14th October 1974. The P7 was initially operated by PD2s but the Corporation bought three Bristol LHS midi-buses in May 1976 and these were used to convert the P7 to 'PAYB' from 30th August and at the same time operate new estate routes to Callon and Grange. The P7 then became service 30 and subsequently services 29 and 31 have also served the estate with the latter being the sole service in 2013 which then continued to Lea. Nos. 242-4 could be considered to have been the pioneer mini-buses and whilst the Callon route lasted barely a year the three Bristols gave more than 10 years service on the other two routes until de-regulation rendered them surplus to requirements. Now carrying the number 342 the first of the trio was fitted with high backed seats and is seen in Birkett Drive on the estate on 7th February 1981. All three were sold to Busways of Newcastle in January 1987 and whilst Nos. 43/4 (their third number) were scrapped a couple of years later No.(3)42 was last recorded in September 1995 working for a private operator on the island of Jersey.

1981 East Lancs-bodied Leyland Atlantean No. 157 is pursued by 1980 Alexander-bodied example No. 148 along Ribbleton Avenue in May 1984. The Department eventually built up a sizeable fleet of Atlanteans, numbering 79 vehicles. No. 157 was retired from service in October 1997 and sold to Thornes of Hemingbrough whilst No. 148 lasted until November 2000 and was one of five of the batch which ended up with local operator J Fishwick & Sons. The last two Alexanders, Nos. 142/3, continued in service until July 2007.

previously stated that it was unlikely to be able to meet the Council's delivery dates. However, the next batch of ten, Nos. 141-50, were bodied by the Scottish firm and all were delivered in February and March 1980. No. 141 was loaned to Lothian Transport, on behalf of Leyland Motors, for two weeks in April 1981. All but two of the remaining 12 PD3s were consequently withdrawn, leaving just Nos. 69 and 70 in service. Nos. 14/5 were both used on a commemorative farewell tour organised by the author, on Sunday 17th February. Not all the PD3s went for scrap; No. 16 was converted for use as a Recovery Vehicle and Nos. 17/9 were modified and used as driver tuition vehicles. Some of the PD3A/1s passed to Lonsdales at Heysham for power station contract work whilst a handful of the type were saved for preservation, including Nos. 2, 5, 14 and 61, although No. 5 donated several parts to No. 2 during the formers restoration at Deepdale throughout 1996 and 1997. The first route to benefit from double-deck 'PAYB' operation using Atlanteans took place on 30th August 1976 when the Ribbleton Gamull Lane (GL) route received an allocation. Consequently, although jointly operated journeys continued to display the route number P5, the route was split at the Bus Station as the Hutton Anchor Inn section remained crew operated. In April 1978 Ribble took over operation of the P5 in exchange for the P2 which reverted to crew operation using the displaced buses from the P5. In October 1976 the P4 was substantially converted to 'PAYB' operation using both Panthers and Atlanteans although some journeys remained crew operated using both Atlanteans and PD3s. Conversion of the PL service followed in August 1978 when the route was extended beyond Queens Drive to a newly constructed turning circle on Sharoe Green Lane, opposite St Claire's church. The Holme Slack service was converted to 'PAYB' operation in January 1980 when another new bus turning circle was commissioned opposite Lily Grove and the P2 was converted for a second time in November which left just the Farringdon Park as a crew operated service which soldiered on until 22nd March 1982 when the last few conductors were retired.

On 3rd November 1980 the route letters, which had been in use since the days of the trams, were replaced by route numbers (see Table 3). The numbers used were taken from the bay numbers which each service used at the Bus Station. One significant route loss was the Lane Ends C, which was replaced by service 33 to Tanterton. On the last day the Lane Ends service was worked by Panther

No. 213 and Atlanteans Nos. 140/9. Panthers Nos. 201/2 were the first of the type to be withdrawn, in September 1980, and both were heavily cannibalised before being sold the following year to PVS at Barnsley, for scrap. Another four were taken off the road before the end of the year. In February 1981 another Leyland Titan demonstrator, NHG 732P, was used on services 7 to Fulwood Row and 26 to Lea.

For the next batch of Atlanteans, which were numbered 151-7, the committee had reverted to East Lancashire for construction of the bodywork and all of the batch were delivered in April 1981. No. 153 arrived at Deepdale painted all white as the base colour for an all-over advert for Slalom Lager. The seven Atlanteans replaced an equal number of Panthers which included the last two of the MCW-bodied batch, Nos. 203/4, with the latter being saved for preservation. As the number of withdrawn Panthers mounted up they were removed from the depot and placed in storage in a warehouse on the docks. All of Nos. 201/3-6/8/10/1/3/5, along with Training Vehicle PD3 No. 17, spent time in storage until August when they were sold. Another eight Atlanteans were received from the Blackburn factory later that year, between October and December. Nos. 158-65 again replaced an equal number of Panthers. Also withdrawn at this time was the last PD3A/1, No. 70. No. 69 had been taken off the road on 16th July, leaving just No. 70 to represent the once large Titan fleet. The latter was used for the last time on Sunday 1st November, when it was

Table 3		
Introduction of Route Numbers – 3rd November 1980		
Service	Letters	Number
Ashton Pedders Lane	A	24
Brookfield via Deepdale Road	BF	36
Broadgate	BR	21
Brookfield via Cromwell Road	CR	35
Tanterton via Brook Street	--	33
Fulwood Circular via Deepdale Road	D	15
Fulwood Circular via North Road	F	20
Farringdon Park	FP	16
Fulwood Row via Deepdale Road	FR	36
Holme Slack	HS	14
Grange Estate	G	12
Ribbleton Gamull Lane	GL	10
Cemetery to Ashton Lane Ends	LEC	98
Longsands Lane via Deepdale Road	LS	36
Moor Nook	MN	7
Fulwood RPH via Plungington Road	PL	22
Frenchwood	P1/P3	29
Larches Estate	P1	27
Lightfoot Lane	P2	28
Lea via Garstang Road	--	26
Lea via Waterloo Road (peak only)	P3	26
Ingol	P4	34
Ingol Redcar Avenue	P6	43
Savick Estate	P7	30

hired by the author for a commemorative tour. Its last duty, however, was made on the afternoon trip to the Continuation Hospital.

The relentless introduction of new Atlanteans continued unabated and Nos. 166-72 were the next to enter service between October and December 1982. The last of the batch, No. 172, was delivered in all-over red as the base colour for a Lion Bitter advert. Some of these vehicles had been affected by a fire at the East Lancashire premises on 22nd May and this incident had delayed their completion. These replaced the last Marshall-bodied Panther, No. 220, and all but one of the 1971 Seddon-bodied batch. The last Atlanteans were received by the undertaking the following summer and were numbered 173-7, 1 and 2. Whereas the first five conformed to the standard specification, Nos. 1 and 2 were different in several ways. Originally, they were to have been conventional buses, numbered 178/9, but it had been decided to obtain two buses with a more up-market appearance which could be used on Private Hires and Excursions. Consequently, the last two were fitted with 74 high backed seats, as opposed to the normal 82 conventional seats. They also only had a single entrance / exit door and were painted in an attractive mainly ivory colour but with three different coloured thin blue bands and had black window surrounds. The side destination displays were not the normal 'built in screen' but oblong boxes attached lower down behind the first window.

One service which was short lived was a route known as the Inner Link which was basically provided for shoppers and was routed around the town centre. Using the service number 13 it ran on Saturdays only from 9th October 1982 to 8th January 1983 using one of the Bristol LHS mini-buses. The last three Panthers in service were renumbered to 33/5/6 in October and they remained in service until August 1984. They were frequent performers on the Larches Estate route and the Continuation Hospital workings. Many of the Panthers were sold to other operators for further service. The Isle of Man National Transport had acquired Nos. 219/21 in January and Nos. 223-5/7/9 in November 1982 and were so impressed with them that they specifically asked to be given first option when more of the type were withdrawn and consequently Nos. 230-3/5/6 also ended up on the island. Most of these returned to the mainland a few years later and joined other former Preston Panthers operating for Citibus of Chadderton, who eventually amassed a grand total of 18 former Preston members of the type which could be seen working into Manchester's Piccadilly Bus Station.

The undertaking's first Olympian was a solitary affair. A33 MRN arrived in February 1984 and, besides carrying the three blue band livery similar to Atlanteans Nos. 1 and 2, it was also adorned with 'Demonstration' lettering for Leyland Vehicles. For some twelve months it was sent to all parts of the UK and could be seen working for operators far and wide. In its early days it was a popular choice for Private Hire and Special Contract work. At the end of 1984 the fleet totalled just 83 vehicles comprising 79 Atlanteans, 3 Bristols and the solitary Olympian.

In June 1983 a new service numbered 37 commenced running via Garstang Road and Watling Street Road to Fulwood Row, which replaced the service which had been routed via Deepdale Road. Twelve months later service 24 to Pedders Lane and service 26 to Lea were both replaced by new service 25 which followed the former's route to Pedders Lane and then continued to Aldfield Avenue at Lea. Services 15 and 20 were extended to Eastway in January 1985 with some journeys further extended to the then new Fulwood Asda store in August of the following year. In February Atlantean No. 164 was loaned to Leyland Vehicles who used it on their test track to assess the performance of the angle drive, following problems encountered with Atlanteans in Singapore. Finally, a number of route re-numberings took place later in the year when the 7 took the number 8 in October and the Brookfield services were re-numbered from 35/36/37 to 5/6/7 the following month.

1965 MCW-bodied Leyland PD3A/1 No. 70 was the last half-cab bus in service with the undertaking and was withdrawn on 1st November 1981. It is seen turning from Deepdale Road into Watling Street Road on 10th July 1981 with an early morning additional journey to Brookfield. The letters had been replaced by route numbers in November 1980 but No. 70 could only display the old nomenclature since the letters and destination were on one single blind. The Farringdon Park FP was the only destination to carry a route number on the last two PD3As, namely 16, on which route they were more usually found.

For many years a lone decker amongst a fleet of Atlanteans, ECW-bodied Leyland Olympian No. 3 was acquired in February 1984 and operated as a demonstrator with Leyland Vehicles for over a year before entering service with the undertaking. It was renumbered twice and was given several changes of livery before being withdrawn at the time of the takeover by Stagecoach in 2009. It is seen at the Ribbleton Gamull Lane terminus in Longridge Road on 24th January 1985 in between demonstration duties.

In the early 1980s the undertaking participated in several large private hire events. On several occasions British Aerospace used large numbers of buses to transport workers to a central meeting venue from their Warton, Samlesbury and Strand Road Works. In May 1982 the Pope visited a number of venues around the country where hundreds of thousands of Catholics congregated at large open venues to hear the pontiff celebrate mass. One such event in the northwest took place at Heaton Park in Manchester on the last day of the month. Vast numbers of buses were used to transport the pilgrims to the event. This view shows what at the time was the southern end of the M66 (now the M60 between J18 and J19) which was closed off to traffic and used as a giant bus park. Eight Preston Atlanteans comprising the complete 1981 batch of Nos. 158-65 made the short trip from the Preston environs. Close inspection reveals that three of the octet are partially visible in this view which is dominated by Ribble Atlanteans and Olympians. In excess of 60 buses are visible in this one view alone and it is unlikely that scenes like this will have ever been repeated on such a grand scale.

Another interesting Private Hire took place on 2nd September 1981 which required 10 vehicles for a British Aircraft Corporation (BAC) outing to Chester. Nine Panthers comprising 1972 Seddon Pennine-bodied Nos. 231/2/3/5/6 and Marshall Camair-bodied Nos. 237/9/40/1 were joined by on-loan Leyland Leopard coach VCW 85V for the trip. Panthers Nos. 231/5/40/1 are seen resting in Chester's Little Roodee coach park.

3. De-regulation and Privatisation

Prior to de-regulation a limited company was set up under the name of 'Preston Borough Transport Limited' with a number of councillors listed as directors. In the months leading up to D-Day, in October 1986, the undertaking had gained several additional school contracts and at that time, apart from the three Bristol LHSs, the fleet consisted entirely of double-deck vehicles. Some of the contracts were unsuitable for double-deckers so four Leyland Nationals, which were numbered 5-8, were acquired from Merseyside PTE to undertake some of the work. They had originally been new to Southport Corporation just before that fleet was absorbed by the PTE in April 1974; indeed YFY 8M was actually delivered new to the PTE. The PTE numbered them 6042/3/8/9 respectively and they had originally been dual-door vehicles with 46 seats but the centre exits were taken out between September 1980 and April 1981. Initially, Preston fitted them with short blinds for school workings only but after only a few months these were replaced with full blinds to enable them to work on ordinary stage services. Alas, No. 6 was written off following an accident in nearby Goosnargh in July 1987. It was only in the summer of 1988 that the three remaining vehicles were eventually repainted into the standard fleet livery. No. 5 was equipped with fittings for towing apparatus and had at least two short spells as the stand-by recovery vehicle whilst the usual incumbent was indisposed. On their withdrawal, in November 1989, the three runners passed to North Western Road Car at Bootle where they returned to their Merseyside haunts. Also at this time Atlanteans Nos. 148/50 went on loan to Yorkshire Traction, working from their Barnsley depot to test out some new road springs.

The undertaking had been preparing for de-regulation and made some route changes immediately from Saturday 25th October. Service 12 to the Grange Estate ran for the last time the day before and service 30 to Savick was converted back to operation with big buses. This spelt the end for the three Bristols and with no specific work for them they were withdrawn the following January. At the same time the Sunday operation of service 5 to Brookfield passed to Mercers Travel of Longridge,

running under contract to LCC. Not surprisingly, the joint operating agreement, which had existed with Ribble for nearly forty years, was terminated. From Saturday 1st November a novel change was made to services 10 from Ribbleton and 16 from Farringdon Park whereby, on that day of the week only, alternate journeys on each service were extended via Fishergate to terminate in Butler Street, alongside the Railway Station. On 8th February 1987 the last Ultimate ticket machines were taken out of use with all buses then fitted with computerised machines. Little competition had so far emerged but this was all about to change.

On 6th April United Transport Buses Ltd commenced a service to the Brookfield Estate using service letter A. Running every five minutes via Deepdale Road, the service was operated by a fleet of brightly painted red and yellow Iveco mini-buses which were innovatively marketed as ZIPPY. This route penetrated into the estate and served roads which had not previously seen a regular bus route. There were no specific stopping places around the estate and passengers could hail the bus to stop at any safe location. Meanwhile, the undertaking prepared to meet the challenge head on and a large batch of 20 Dodge mini-buses with 22-seat Northern Counties-built bodies, which were numbered 50-69 (67 had 20 high backed seats), had been hastily ordered and the first 12 were all delivered on the 15th April. These were intended for a new service, numbered 19, to the Royal Preston Hospital (RPH) and for the conversion of services 27 to Larches and 30 to Savick. All three services commenced formal operation on the 21st (they also ran the day before as a trial without collecting any fares) operating to frequent timetables and incorporating sections of route which applied the 'Hail & Ride' principle. Despite the introduction of mini-buses on the Larches service, Atlanteans continued to be used on the original service which ran in parallel. Although retaining the same number, service 30 was substantially re-routed via Wellfield Road and Tulketh Road, instead of Fylde Road and Tulketh Brow. In preparation for the introduction of the new mini-buses the undertaking had taken three buses on loan from other operators for driver familiarisation. These were Freight Rover Dormobile-bodied D861/2 LWR, from Yorkshire Rider at Leeds, and D912 NBA, a Dodge S56 from Northern Counties.

Apart from No. 67, the remainder of the batch were delivered before the end of the month. These

Just prior to bus de-regulation, in August 1986, four Leyland Nationals were purchased from the Merseyside PTE. The crumpled front of accident damaged Leyland National No. 6 contrasts sharply with No. 8. This view was taken in September 1987, two months after the accident. No. 6 was subsequently sold to Burnley & Pendle Transport for spares.

After running in their 'as acquired' MPTE colours for some two years the three survivors were painted into the fleet livery of blue & ivory in January and August 1988. No. 5 had two spells deputising as the recovery vehicle and it is seen during its second spell parked in the standby location in November 1988. Note the orange flasher on the roof. Behind is one of the two higher spec Atlanteans and at the side of the bus is Preston North End's Team Coach which at the time was a 1970 Plaxton-bodied Leyland Leopard. All three Nationals were withdrawn in November 1989 and sold to the North Western Road Car Co.

Following the introduction of their services to Brookfield, Larches and Lea in April, United Transport introduced two further services from 4th May 1987, lettered E and F, which both ran to the Moor Nook estate. These ran in direct competition to Preston's service 8. This picture, taken on13th July 1987, depicts 'Zippy' Peugeot Talbot tri-axle Pullman No.070 departing for Moor Nook with Preston Atlantean No. 140 behind on competing service 8 which is somewhat significant as the service was actually converted to mini-bus operation on this date.

Another operator to take advantage of the opportunities presented by bus deregulation was local operator Mercers Travel who were based at nearby Longridge. Mercers commenced running two services from the Bus Station, namely the M1 to Longridge and the M2 to Gamull Lane both of which competed with Preston's service 11. Seen parked out of service in Lytham Road on 23rd April 1989 is former South Yorkshire Fleetline OKW 518R.

In May 1987 a Duple-bodied Leyland Tiger was purchased for Private Hire, Tour and Excursion work. Originally numbered 40, it was re-registered and renumbered to 309 in March 1995. The Tiger was replaced by a Volvo B10M in March 2003 when it was sold on to local operator Bon Chaunce Coaches.

In 1987 a total of 31 Dodge mini-buses with Northern Counties, mainly 22-seat bodies (Nos. 44, 67, 70/1 had 20 seats), were hurriedly pressed into service to combat United Transport's Zippy operations. The first to enter service were Nos. 50-6 on 20th April. No. 56 is seen in Thorntrees Avenue Lea in February 1989.

included two of the narrower bodied S46 type, Nos. 68/9, which were also used as driver tuition vehicles. United Transport also introduced their next services on 20th April, running to Larches (B) and Lea (C) via Tulketh Brow and Ashton Lane Ends, the day before the Preston services officially commenced. On 4th May two more frequent new Zippy services commenced running to Moor Nook, which were denoted by the letters E and F and encircled the estate in opposite directions. The combined frequency of these services provided for a five minute interval service. Meanwhile, Preston introduced another new service on 11th May which duplicated the existing Holme Slack route but ran beyond the latter's terminus, via Ronaldsway and Lambert Road, to Fairfax Road. To distinguish this service from the 14 it ran using the route number 114 and a couple of months later it replaced the 14 in the evenings and on Sunday. At the end of the month all journeys on the Larches service were converted to mini-bus operation. On the same date Zippy service G commenced running the short distance to Peel Hall Street.

Several more Dodge mini-buses duly arrived, with Nos. 70/1 being delivered on 23rd May and Nos. 41-3, 72-4 appearing in late June. Private Hire work had generally been sufficiently covered by normal bus types in the fleet. However, in April it was decided to branch out and enter the Tours market. D40 AFV, a Duple-bodied Leyland Tiger, was originally ordered by Ulsterbus but it ended up being acquired by Preston and entered service on 15th May, when it was used by PNE FC. A few days earlier Plaxton-bodied Leyland Tiger, B417 CMC, was hired from Blackburn Borough Transport to cover a specific Private Hire commitment. No. 40, (later renumbered 309), gave reliable service with the undertaking for nearly 16 years, during which time it changed its identity once and livery style twice. The original livery was based on the double-deck version of the three blue band layout. More Zippy services were inaugurated in June with service D to Cadley Causeway and service H to Tanterton, both running via the Plungington Road corridor, commencing on the 1st of the month. Two weeks later Zippy service I commenced running to Fishwick Parade via New Hall Lane.

From 4th July alternate departures on service 22 to the RPH were re-numbered to 23 and extended to run via Sherwood Way and Eastway to Fulwood Asda. A few days later, on the 13th, Preston Bus

initiated a substantial round of service changes. The Brookfield services were rationalised whereby services 5 and 6 were both withdrawn and service 7 was converted to operation by mini-buses. Service 8 to Moor Nook was also converted to mini-bus operation and substantially re-routed via Ribbleton Avenue and Ribbleton Hall Drive, thereby leaving Miller Road to be served by the two Zippy routes. All service 10 journeys were re-numbered to 11, with the full service subsequently operating via the Grange Estate, and at the same time the through journeys on both the 10(11) and 16 to the Railway Station were discontinued. Changes also took place to the Ingol and Tanterton services with service 28 being re-numbered to 32. United Transport only made one change to their services on the same date, with the Brookfield service being linked to the Larches and Lea services. To counter the alteration to service 8 made by Preston Bus, from 27th July United Transport commenced a third service to Moor Nook (G), running in direct competition via Ribbleton Avenue and at the same time they withdrew the Peel Hall Street service. From the beginning of August service I was replaced by extending service D beyond the Bus Station to Fishwick Parade.

Whereas United Transport were for the time being content with consolidating their new operations, Preston Bus made several more route alterations before the end of the year. On 17th August another new service was inaugurated, using service number 24, which ran to Conway Drive in Fulwood. It was only operated off-peak and required just one bus. Dodge No. 44 was the dedicated vehicle and had two fewer seats and a luggage pen for passengers' shopping. Alas, the service was lightly used and ran for the last time on 9th October. Five Atlanteans, Nos. 102/4-7, had been withdrawn at the start of the summer school holidays and were advertised for sale. The Liverpool based company, North Western Road Car, was keen to obtain the buses and asked that No. 103 was also included in the sale to complete the numerical run. The buses all departed on 16th September.

The Zippy routes had now penetrated all parts of the town but United Transport had seen a need to rationalise the network and from 20th September all the services were completely recast using 'Z' prefixed service numbers, as opposed to letters, which included some out-of-town services to nearby areas which had been started in competition with

1980 Alexander-bodied Leyland Atlantean No. 142 is seen in Abingdon Street, Blackpool town centre in July 1988, setting out back for Preston on the inter-town service which ran for several months in 1987 in response to Blackpool Transport's services 165 & 180/2 which ran into Preston. This batch of Alexanders had cash trays fitted to enable change to be given and were the usual weekday performers on the 39.

Seen inside the dockshop in February 1989 surrounded by a plethora of mini-buses and Atlanteans is Northern Counties-bodied Renault S56 No. 75 which was one of a batch of three which were new in February 1988. Twenty one of this type were eventually operated but only the first six received, Nos. 75-7 and 47-9 had the 'PRESTON' outline name on the bonnet. These were removed in 1990 when the vehicles were first repainted and replaced with the standard 'Preston Mini' fleet name. No. 75 survived until September 1995 when it was sold to R W Appleby of Conisholme for further service.

Considering they were only supposed to have a shelf life of around 5 to 6 years, many of the Dodge and Renault mini-buses achieved nearly twice that number of years with the undertaking. Northern Counties-bodied Nos. 69 and 79 are seen climbing Leighton Street on 5th July 1991. Service 27 was re-routed only a few days earlier in consequence of the right turn from Marsh Lane into Wellfield Road being no longer possible due to the rebuilding of the former road as a dual carriageway. The route was withdrawn in October 2006 when it was predominantly replaced by the Orbit services although the latter subsequently followed a much different route.

Number 85 was one of a batch of ten Northern Counties-bodied Renault S56 mini-buses which entered service in April and May 1988 and which were principally used to expand services to out-lying areas such as Penwortham, Longton and Bamber Bridge. This view is taken at the top of Friargate in April 1989 by which time only mini-bus operated services were routed this way. No. 85 took part in the 1992 Guild Trades Procession and was one of several of the type replaced by Metroriders in September 1995. It was sold to Bandwagon of Edinburgh for further service.

Ribble. The town services ran at frequent intervals, on headways which varied between 5 minutes and 10 minutes, whilst the out-of-town services ran to a 12 minute frequency.

There were now some 75 Zippy mini-buses, comprising Ivecos, Freight Rover Sherpas and Talbot-Pullmans, plying their trade on the town's streets. United Transport only had the use of a minimal number of bays at the Bus Station and to see two or three buses parked on one bay was normal practice. Preston Bus continued to make service alterations to ensure that United Transport didn't steal a march on them and on 12th October service 6 to Brookfield, which operated via Deepdale Road, was reinstated using mini-buses. Two more Dodges, Nos. 45/6, were obtained to enable the change to take place and these were the last mini-buses to enter the fleet for several months. From 9th November another new service commenced operation. Service 31 was an infrequent service which was mainly operated by Atlanteans and was routed out via the A6 to Broughton and then returned via Woodplumpton village to the Bus Station. To complete the service alterations throughout a very busy year service 114 was re-routed to serve Romford Road, from 14th November.

There then followed a relatively quiet few months as both operators took stock of the situation. United Transport had undoubtedly attracted passengers, but predominantly at the expense of Preston Bus. They were not the only operator to take advantage of the open market as several other operators had also introduced competing services, although some of these were levelled more at Ribble's passenger base. Greater Manchester Transport worked the 118 service from Wigan to Preston and Blackpool Transport operated services 180/2 from Poulton and Fleetwood and service 165 from Blackpool, with the former producing AEC Swifts, Dennis Lancets and Leyland Nationals and the latter bringing green and cream Atlanteans on a regular basis to Preston. Mercers Travel of Longridge also had a short spell operating competing services on the Ribbleton Lane corridor to Longridge (M1), where they were based, and Ribbleton (M2). Ribble also commenced two local routes running to Lea (168) and Tanterton (169). Meanwhile, Preston Bus had ordered more mini-buses for delivery in early 1988, to enable the undertaking to counter United Transport by starting up a number of competing services on the out-of-town routes. In total, 16 Renault mini-buses

with 25-seat Northern Counties-built bodies were received between February and May, comprising Nos. 47-9 and 75-87. However, United Transport sold their Preston and Manchester operations to Ribble in March and whilst a number of routes were withdrawn, particularly the out-of-town services, competition continued to some areas of the town.

No time was wasted in putting the new buses into service. On 11th April service 5 to Brookfield was reinstated; services 21 to Broadgate and 29 to Frenchwood both gained the use of mini-buses and a new service, numbered 43, commenced running to Ingol with mini-buses and operating via Brook Street and Mill Lane. A few weeks later, on 16th May, two new services commenced running to Bamber Bridge and Penwortham, with service numbers 17 and 4 respectively. The existing destination blinds in the Atlanteans were extended with the addition of an insert, which contained the place names of many nearby towns. This was quite appropriate as the undertaking decided to turn its attention towards Blackpool Transport and from 16th July a service commenced running to Blackpool, via the M55 motorway. Using the service number 39 it was a joint venture with Lancaster City Transport, although wholly operated by Preston, almost exclusively using Atlanteans from the 141-50 batch as these buses were fitted with cash trays to enable change to be given. On Sunday one of the Renaults would be used as these were also fitted with trays for use on out-of-town services. The Blackpool service was withdrawn two weeks after the end of the seaside resort's illuminations period.

Another three Renaults arrived in November, numbered 88-90, but throughout the year no buses were withdrawn. Preston Bus made two final route changes before deciding that no more changes were necessary. In February 1989, the Bamber Bridge service was extended a short distance from the Hob Inn to a new Sainsburys Supermarket and, from 15th May, the last new route commenced running to Longton with service number 3. Another two Renaults, Nos. 91/2, completed the mini-bus revolution with some 52 of the type then in service. Attention was now turned to replacing more of the ageing Atlanteans and a small batch of four Leyland Lynx, Nos. 10-3, entered the fleet in March, replacing the remaining four of the first batch of Alexander-bodied Atlanteans, Nos. 101/8-10, all of which were eventually sold to Hyndburn Borough Transport. The first two Lynx were fitted

Leyland Lynx No. 11 was one of four of the type which entered service in March 1989 replacing the last four of the 1974/5 Alexander-bodied Atlanteans, Nos. 101/8-10. A further eleven Lynx joined the fleet the following year and No. 11 is seen climbing Adelphi Street in typical January weather conditions in its first full winter of operation. It was withdrawn in September 2006 and exported to Malta where it saw a few more years of active service. Service 33 was the initial route to Tanterton which was inaugurated on 3rd November 1980 but it was withdrawn after 28th July 2007 leaving route 35, which operated via Fylde Road, to serve the area.

New in April 1991 No. 102 is seen later that year passing the old covered market in Lancaster Road. One of a batch of four Northern Counties-bodied Leyland Olympians, all four were still in service in 2013 and were repainted into the new PB Rotala livery. Service 25 was withdrawn by Stagecoach in March 2009 and was effectively replaced by their 68 service which ran to Blackpool. The adjacent market building took several years to come to fruition as the original structure collapsed during construction in August 1870; it was finally completed in 1875.

During the 1992 Preston Guild week this open-top ELC-bodied Atlantean was hired from Lancaster City Transport and, besides performing special duties, was used on normal stage services 16 to Farringdon Park and 33 to Tanterton. New in September 1972 it started life as No. 84 in the Blackburn Corporation Transport fleet before passing to Lancaster in the mid-1980s. It is seen in Woodplumpton Road on 1st September heading back to town but seemingly with few or no passengers onboard. The building behind, with the corrugated roof, was originally the Viking Motors bus garage which was later owned by a brewery and latterly by a Funeral Director.

At certain times during the 1992 Preston Guild week the main town centre streets were closed to traffic whilst the large processions took place. A handful of mini-bus routes terminated on the Railway Station Approach Road during the road closures. 1987 Northern Counties-bodied Dodge S56 No. 73 waits on the Savick service whilst on loan Optare Metrorider demonstrator J363 BNW can be seen on the Larches service. The fleet reached its maximum ever size at this time, standing at 132 buses, and in addition there were three buses on loan during Guild week. This view was taken on 3rd September.

1992 Leyland Olympians Nos. 109/10 lay over at the Bus Station in July 1994 between duties on the school holiday leisure centre services. Service 89 ran from Lea to Fulwood Leisure Centre and the 88 ran from Farringdon Park to West View (originally Fulwood) Leisure Centre. They were operated on behalf of LCC every year except three between 1981 and 1999. This bus was one of the two Olympians specially painted by Rotala for the 2012 Guild.

The balance of an order for ten Optare Metroriders, Nos. 5-10, were delivered in March 1995. All were received without the blue relief which was applied at the depot. However, whereas Nos. 5-7 didn't enter service until they were completed, the other three ran for around a month without the blue. No. 8 is seen in Whitby Avenue on the Ingol estate in April 1995.

with 47 bus seats whilst all subsequent vehicles of the type had 45 high backed seats. Nos. 10/2 spent short spells out on loan to Blackpool Transport and Leyland Vehicles respectively.

Another new vehicle which was received at the same time was Northern Counties-bodied Olympian, F32 AHG, which had 85 seats and was numbered 32. A further batch of Lynx numbered 14-8 was received in November and the five new buses replaced the three remaining Nationals and the first East Lancs-bodied Atlanteans to be withdrawn, Nos. 113/5/8. In April Ribble became one of Stagecoach's early acquisitions and a number of service alterations were made, which reduced the competition level to more or less the pre-April 1987 level. Whilst Stagecoach Ribble withdrew the remaining Zippy town services, Preston Bus similarly withdrew their the out-of-town services, but at the same time introduced mini-bus services 9 to Moor Nook and 31 to Savick, which filled the gaps left by the withdrawal of the Zippy routes on Miller Road and Brook Street respectively. At the same time a new service to Tanterton, numbered 35, started running via Fylde Road using Atlanteans. March 1990 saw the arrival of a batch of four Leyland-bodied Olympians which were numbered 34-7. Whilst Nos. 34/5 were fitted with 72 high backed seats the other two were fitted with 78 ordinary bus seats. In November 1990 a further six Lynx, Nos. 23/4/6-9, joined the fleet. No. 27 was taken on a two week Aid Mission trip to Romania at the end of September 1992, when it was reduced to 25 seats to make room for the aid parcels. Whereas Private Hire work was not unusual for the type, No. 28 deputised for the failed AFC Bournemouth team coach on 3rd September 1991, when it took the players and officials (Harry Redknapp was the Cherries manager at the time) back to Bournemouth after a match at Deepdale and No. 27 made the trip to Wembley on 28th May 1994 carrying PNE supporters to the League 3 Play-Off final against Wycombe Wanderers. Twelve more Atlanteans were withdrawn throughout the year with four of the type going to Warrington Borough Transport and the remainder to the fledgling Yorkshire operator, Sheffield Omnibus.

Four second-hand Dodge mini-buses were acquired in January 1991 to work the newly won Portway Park

& Ride contract service. These consisted of three ELC-bodied vehicles from Stagecoach, which had originally operated with Barrow Borough Transport, and a Reeve Burgess-bodied machine which had been new to Cumberland. They were numbered 6-9 in the Preston fleet. Nos. 8 and 9 initially carried all-over advert liveries, whilst No. 6 entered service in all-white, before finally gaining a unique Park & Ride colour scheme. These were followed by four Northern Counties-bodied Olympians, Nos. 101-4, in April and a further eight, Nos. 106-10/2-4, with Workington-built Leyland bodies, twelve months later. No. 106 was used by Leyland Vehicles as a demonstrator before entering service with Preston, whilst No. 107 was exhibited at the Bus & Coach Exhibition in Birmingham on 14th October 1991 and was painted in a specially adapted livery for the 1992 Preston Guild. Nos. 107/14 had 72 high back seats whilst the other six had 78 bus seats. The remaining Atlanteans through to No. 140 were all withdrawn and passed to Sheffield Omnibus for further service. The latter operator based its livery on the Preston livery on account of having acquired so many buses from the undertaking. At the end of 1991 the fleet had reached its maximum ever size, which totalled 132 vehicles.

Since the competition with United Transport had ceased there had been very few service changes of any significance. A new mini-bus service, numbered 29, to Savick had commenced on 28th January 1991, running on Monday to Friday peak times only; whilst service 10 began running to the Grange estate on 10th December 1992 with no evening or Sunday service being provided. During Guild week, in September 1992, open top Atlantean UBV 84L was taken on loan from Lancaster City Transport and was used in normal service on the Farringdon Park and Tanterton routes. The same month saw the appearance of the first destination blinds showing yellow lettering instead of white. The replacement of the original blinds took many years to complete with buses only being treated on an 'as required' basis. In fact, a handful of the old

Table 4			
Registration	Type	Owner	Dates in Use
H401 DMJ	Renault S75, R Burgess B29F	Renault, Dunstable	11/6/91-19/6/91
H398 SYG	Optare Metrorider B29F	Optare, Leeds	28/6/91-4/7/91
J363 BNW	Optare Metrorider B23F	Optare, Leeds	1/9/92-8/9/92
K112 SRH	Dennis Dart, Plaxton B34F	London Buses Ltd	15/9/93-23/9/93
L836 MWT	Optare Metrorider B29F	Optare, Leeds	21/4/94-29/4/94
L708 LKY	Mercedes Benz, Wright B29F	Mercedes, Barnsley	3/8/94-15/8/94

blinds were still in use on some of the Olympians in 2013. Whilst no new buses were received in 1993, none were withdrawn either. The significant event of the year was the privatisation of the undertaking on 1st April, following a management and employee buyout, with the newly formed company being known as 'Preston Transport Holdings Ltd'.

With a predicted design life of only 5 to 6 years for the Dodge mini-buses, various alternatives for their replacement were looked at (see Table 4). Following various trials it was decided that the Metrorider would be the most suitable vehicle to replace the ageing fleet of Dodges and Renaults. A total of 40 of the type were put into service in several batches over a period of 3½ years. Whilst numerically the first 16 were of the 25-seat variety the rest had 29 seats. The first four, Nos. 1-4, were dedicated to the Portway Park & Ride service and directly replaced the acquired Dodges in December 1994. A batch of ten had been ordered but the remaining six weren't delivered until the following March. All ten were delivered without the blue relief and, although this was applied in the company's own paintshop within a few weeks, Nos. 8-10 actually saw a few weeks service in their 'as delivered' state. Although some subsequent vehicles were also delivered without the blue, none of the others ran in this condition.

The next to be received were eight of the longer version, Nos. 20-7, which took over operation of service 19 on 2nd October 1995. This was somewhat unusual as normally vehicles were put into service on an 'as ready' basis. Following completion of the order in March 1996 with Nos. 28-31, another six 25-seat buses, numbered 11-6, followed that October. The remaining twelve, Nos. 17-9 and 32-40 followed over the next two years with the last two, Nos. 39 and 40, replacing Nos. 3 and 4 on the Park & Ride service. Finally, two earlier models were acquired from Blackburn Transport in November 2000 and given fleet numbers 41 and 42. These were fitted with 26 seats and had started life with London Transport in August 1991. The Blackburn green was over painted with blue whilst additionally No. 41 carried an all-over vinyl advert which was left on the vehicle. These two had been bought as a stop-gap measure and were the first Metroriders to be withdrawn in December 2002. The new Metroriders replaced some 43 of the 56 original Dodge/Renault mini-buses, leaving just Nos. 51/4, 61/2/4, 72/3/7 and 88-92 to soldier on.

Following their withdrawal, most of the mini-buses, or 'breadvans' as they became affectionately known, found gainful employment elsewhere. One exception, following it's withdrawal for the second time in October 1996, was No. 58 which was stripped of reusable parts and then reduced to a pile of scrap before being removed in a skip. Similarly, No. 52 was also sold for scrap, to a local dealer. No. 44, which was bought by a concern in London, subsequently appeared in several film and TV clips whilst No. 71 was acquired by a man of the cloth and was relocated to the Isle of Tiree in Scotland. No. 45 was stripped of its seats and the glazing removed and replaced with panelwork, before being sold to Cottage Nurseries of Newark for use as a van to transport plants. Warrington Borough Transport took ten of the earlier examples with a number being repainted before dispatch. Nos. 53/5-7 were painted yellow and blue in April 1995, whilst Nos. 46 and 67 were given a coat of red and white before following in October. The other four, Nos. 43, 50, 60 and 74, were taken in April 1996 and were not repainted before sale. Similarly, Nos. 6, 9 and 65 were painted white in early 1995 for their new owner, the Lincolnshire Road Car Co.

In February and March several buses were re-numbered to create distinct groupings. Olympians, Nos. 32-7, were renumbered to 132-7; the Lynx were re-numbered en-bloc with the addition of 200 to their numbers and the coach was numbered 309, to correspond with its newly acquired registration PRN 909. Consequently, mini-buses were now numbered between 1-99, double-deckers between 100-99 and single-deckers between 200-99 whilst the coach had a number in the 300 series. Lynx No. 229 emerged from the bodyshop in August, considerably modified from its original appearance. Apart from the sale of Alexander-bodied Atlantean No. 146 to Lincolnshire Road Car in November, no further Atlanteans had been retired from service for a period of five years, since No. 140 had been withdrawn in June 1992. Withdrawals of the type recommenced in October 1997, when Nos. 152-5/7/8 were taken out of service, although Nos. 152/8 were both reinstated for further use the following year being replaced by Nos. 151/60 on the disposal list.

On 27th October 1997 the first route changes for some time were implemented. Service 14 was converted to mini-bus operation and extended to Fairfax Road. In May 2001 the parallel service 114 was withdrawn, with all journeys henceforth

This Van Hool-bodied Volvo B10M was bought at auction in February 2003 and replaced the 1987 Leyland Tiger. It retained its 'as acquired' turquoise livery throughout its service with the company and was sold in September 2006 following a decision to wind up the coaching side of the business. Fleet number 323 was never actually carried and it was the third bus to carry the registration PRN 909 which was then passed to Scania No. 200. Seen in No. 3 garage this view dates from December 2005.

1998 Optare Metrorider No. 36 is seen in April 2006 being cleaned out for another spell of duty. No. 36 was one of the last six of the type which were still in operation at the takeover by Stagecoach. It continued in service until mid-March 2009 and was then placed in store at Lillyhall until the following February when all six were sold to PVS at Barnsley.

operating as service 14. Additionally, service 32 to Tanterton was also converted to mini-bus operation and a new service, numbered 36, commenced running to Cottam. In September 1998 Atlantean No. 176 was turned out in a commemorative livery of maroon with three cream bands, just prior to an open day which was held at the depot on the 27th. The colours of mid-blue and ivory had adorned Preston's buses for over 30 years and the Managing Director had decided that a new brighter image was required. Consequently, in April 1999, Olympian No. 107 was used as a canvass to develop a new blue and cream colour scheme.

As the Transport Authority, Lancashire County Council was keen to encourage local operators to work in partnership with them to introduce buses to their fleets which provided easy access for all prospective passengers, including wheelchair users and parents with young children. Consequently, the term 'Quality Bus Route' was coined for this new initiative. In the twelve months from May 1998 Preston Bus trialled a number of demonstrators (see Table 5), all of which were evaluated on service 11 to Ribbleton. In the event it was not the low-floor single-decker which was to make its debut on the streets of Preston but a double-deck model in the shape of the Dennis Trident. No. 190 was delivered on 26th November 1999 and was the first of a batch of seven Tridents to be used to convert the Tanterton services, 33 and 35, to low-floor bus operation. Following trials with Olympian No. 110 to determine a suitable livery style, Nos. 190-6 introduced an attractive colour scheme to the fleet which incorporated route branding transfers. No. 190 was the only one of the batch to be fitted with high backed seats on the lower deck. Their introduction was well publicised and Nos. 190/2/3 were displayed on the Market Square beforehand. The bus stops on the two routes were the first in a long programme to be altered with a raised up section, which married the levels of the pavement and the lowered position of the bus entrance platform which, with the aid of a fold out platform,

provided easy access for all passengers. Six of the batch went into service on 13th December with the seventh, No. 194, following the day after.

Initially the conversion of routes 22/3 was to have been a gradual process and only six more Tridents were ordered. However, this was subsequently changed to eleven which were numbered 182-9/97-9 and the first three to enter service were Nos. 183/4/6 on 31st October 2000, albeit on other services. This batch differed in having electronic blinds, including side destination and rear number apertures. Only seven out of the 11 had route branding transfers applied, with Nos. 189/97-9 left blank. No. 186 was unfortunately involved in an accident on its first day out and had to return to Blackburn for repairs. The Tridents were fitted with two piece folding doors and these initially proved to be a constant source of problems requiring frequent attention from the manufacturers. They replaced an equal number of Atlanteans which left only 14 of the type in service. As was usual with retired Preston buses, all 18 moved on to other operators for further service. These included Nos. 144/7/8/50, which passed to J Fishwick & Sons in November 2000, followed by No. 149 in January 2001. Not only did they gain a new lease of life but they looked superb, painted in Fishwick's two-tone green livery. Four of the East Lancs-bodied vehicles, Nos. 169/71/81/2, were painted red and white for Lloyds of Bagillt, whilst No. 141 was bought for preservation.

In partnership with LCC, service 19 was the first mini-bus operated route to be given Quality Bus status, in January 2002. First inaugurated in April 1987, the service was initially operated by Dodge mini-buses which were then followed by new Metroriders. The first of a third generation of mini-buses, Optare Solos Nos. 51-8, were all received in December 2001 and the route branding for the 19 was applied at the depot. Four of the batch were used on the Portway Park & Ride service over the Christmas break before settling in on their intended duties. They had electronic front and side destination / number screens and rear number only screens. They were also fitted with camera displays in the cab area for rear and entrance viewing. Besides being of low-floor configuration they were similarly fitted with a platform ramp, which could be extended onto the pavement to accept

Table 5			
Registration	Type	Owner	Dates in Use
R98 HUA	Optare Excel B42F	Optare, Leeds	15/4/98-4/5/98.
R32 GNW	DAF SB220, Plaxton B36F	DAF	11/5/98-1/6/98
R739 TMO	Dennis Dart, Plaxton B38F	Plaxton, Scarborough	18/5/98-27/5/98
R460 VOP	Volvo B10BLE, Wright B36F	Volvo Buses, Warwick	10/6/98-25/6/98
R280 SDT	Mercedes Benz, UVG B43F	Mercedes, Tankersley	10/7/98-27/7/98
S350 SET	Scania, Wright B39F	Scania, Worksop	23/10/98-6/11/98

In 2003 four of the later style of Leyland Lynx were acquired from Halton Transport at Widnes. The first two arrived on 11th April and were Nos. 52 & 64 in the Halton fleet, becoming Nos. 221/2 in the Preston fleet. Nos. 58/9 followed on 29th July, becoming Preston Nos. 219/20. As can be seen from the above view taken in the bodyshop they arrived in complete Halton livery, still retaining fleet names and numbers, and were repainted at Deepdale. Unfortunately, they proved to be very unreliable machines and all of Nos. 219-21 saw barely ten months of service before being disposed of. No. 222, however, wasn't withdrawn until August 2006.

Former Lothian Buses Alexander-bodied Leyland Olympians Nos. 126/8 are seen passing through Biggar High Street on delivery from Edinburgh to Preston on 19th April 2005. These were the last pair of ten buses which were acquired in March and April. The buses were repainted at Lothian's Marine depot but were taken directly to S & T at Blackburn to have the centre doors removed before entering service with the company.

push or wheelchairs. The platform area at the front contained three individual tip-up seats. Nos. 59-67 were added to the fleet in November, following the acquisition of a new contract to operate the already existing Portway and the new Capitol Centre Park & Ride services. Again supported by LCC, the contract specified that the colours worn by the vehicles should be distinctive and lilac was proposed as an alternative to the cream. They were basically the same as the first batch, except that they were fitted with air-conditioning and double-glazed windows. All but No. 67 entered service on the first two days of December 2002 with the latter following on the 6th.

With regards to the remaining Dodge / Renault mini-buses, No. 91 was written off in an accident in December 1999 and No. 62 followed No. 44 to Greenhill Plant Hire in south London. It subsequently starred in an ITV drama called 'A line in the sand' in which production it was blown up. Nos. 61 and 77 were withdrawn in May 2001 and No. 92 was another write off, in September. Five more, Nos. 51/4, 72/3 and 88 were retired in December and the last three, Nos. 64, 89 and 90 finally bowed out on 4th January 2002. Nos. 51/4 were renumbered to 510 and 540 respectively, only three weeks before they were withdrawn to accommodate the new Solos. In February 2003, a Volvo B10M with a Van Hool 53-seat coach body, T894 HBF, was bought at auction to replace the Tiger coach. It had previously worked from new for the Potteries operator, Bassetts Coachways. Shortly after its entry into service, on 1st March 2003, it received the registration PRN 909 (originally carried by MCW PD3/4 No. 17) which was transferred from the Tiger. The number 323 originated from the auction LOT number and was used for computer records only. Also, in February, Metroriders Nos. 9 and 10 were the first of the type received new to be withdrawn.

In April two Mark 2 Leyland Lynx were acquired from Halton Borough Transport. Numbered 221/2 they were followed by two more

examples, Nos. 219/20, in July. All four were received in 'as withdrawn condition' and were repainted at Deepdale. However, they were found to be in poor mechanical condition and all except No. 222 lasted little over 12 months in service with the company. At the same time another seven Metroriders were taken out of service and sold to other operators. Adverts had first been placed on the sides of Preston's Corporation buses in 1952. Often the removal of the adverts would cause damage to the paintwork. However, in 2005, the Olympians and Tridents were fitted with advert frames which enabled the adverts to be slotted into place in sections, and similarly removed, thus eliminating the likelihood of any damage.

No new buses were received in 2004 and the fleet then numbered 115 buses. The reliability of some of the remaining Atlanteans was now giving some cause for concern. Consequently, a batch of ten Alexander-bodied Olympians was purchased from Lothian Buses. The buses were painted into Preston colours at the Edinburgh operator's Marine depot and collected by Preston drivers, two at a time, as follows:- Nos. 127/30 on 8th March, Nos. 125/31 on 15th March, Nos. 129/32 on 22nd March, Nos. 123/4 on 5th April and finally Nos. 126/8 on the 19th April. On delivery they were taken directly to a bus bodywork specialist firm in Blackburn to have the centre exit doors removed. They were primarily for use on school contract work but were frequent performers on normal stage services. No. 130 was later fitted with seat belts for use on a specific schools contract. Six of the remaining 14 Atlanteans, Nos. 152/8/9/65/8/70, were replaced on school work, with all but No. 165 making the long journey to Inverness having been acquired by Scotbus. Alas, No. 158 lost its roof under a low bridge after only a few months in service with its new operator. Meanwhile, No. 165 was painted green and white for local operator Bon Chaunce. The scene was now set for what was to be the company's final Act.

Between 2001 and 2008 a number of preserved buses received attention at the depot. However Leyland TD4/ Beadle OKP 980, owned by Thornes of Hemingbrough, spent almost six years in the workshops during which time it was completely rebuilt before being painted into its original Maidstone & District colours. It was finally completed in April 2006 when this view was taken.

4. Stagecoach and Rotala

Prior to the onslaught mounted by Stagecoach, Preston Bus had made a substantial investment in new low-floor vehicles. In 2004 no new vehicles had entered the fleet and the following year new vehicles had again been at a premium, with the main acquisition being one of 10 seventeen year old Olympians from Lothian Buses to replace some of the even older Atlanteans on school contract work. However, in December 2005, the company received a token number of three 32-seat Solos from Optare, which were part of an eventual order for 17 such buses intended for use on the new proposed Orbit circular services. The introduction of these new services was delayed several times, mainly because the interested parties couldn't come to an agreement on the final routing. In the latter months of the year several demonstrators were trialled on service 11, to Ribbleton Gamull Lane, as the company looked for a suitable low-floor single deck bus to replace the ageing Lynx (see Table 6).

From the seven buses operated the Scania

3rd March 2007. Meanwhile, Nos. 210/6 passed to Scotbus of Inverness. Also, in September, the company opted out of the coach tour business and the Volvo coach was sold to an operator near York.

The following month saw the arrival of a number of new Solos. Nos. 68-76 were of the 8.5m long version with seating for 28 passengers, whilst Nos. 84-91 were the 9.2m long variant with 32 seats and were intended for the long-awaited Orbit routes. These were all painted in a version of the new livery of blue, ivory and lime green. At the same time Nos. 81-3, which were delivered in the former livery, were sent to Bus S & T (later known as Bus & Coach World) in Blackburn to be repainted in the new colours. The Orbit routes eventually commenced running from Sunday 22nd October and as a direct consequence services 5 (Longsands), 6 (Brookfield), 27 and 127 (Larches) and 43 (Ingol) were all withdrawn. The influx of the new mini-buses resulted in the withdrawal of 13 Metroriders, all of which were bought by Caledonia Buses of Glasgow. At the turn of the year two East Lancs-bodied Scania Omnidekkas, Nos. 151/2, entered the fleet. It appeared that these had originally been ordered by another operator and each bus had a different colour of seat moquette.

Table 6

Registration	Type	Owner	Dates in Use
BX05 UVZ	Mercedes Benz Citaro B42F	Evobus, Coventry	5/5/05-17/5/05
YN54 OCJ	Scania Omnidekka H80F	Scania, Worksop	23/8/05-6/9/05
YJ55 BLX	Optare Tempo X1200 B42F	Optare, Leeds	31/10/05-7/11/05
YN55 RCY	Scania OmniCity B42F	Scania, Worksop	4/11/05-21/11/05
BV55 UAZ	Volvo B7RLE, Wright B44F	Volvo Buses, Warwick	28/11/05-14/12/05
SN54 HXG	Alexander Dennis Enviro 300 B44F	Alexander, Falkirk	30/11/05-13/12/05
BX05 UWG	Mercedes Benz Citaro B42F	Evobus, Coventry	30/11/05-8/12/05

had impressed the most and seven of the N94UB chassis type, with East Lancashire Esteem low-floor bodies, were ordered for delivery in 2006. They arrived in August with PL06 registration marks, and whilst Nos. 201/2 were used on the road for driver familiarisation, the remainder did not enter service until September and were subsequently re-registered with PO56 marks. These buses were primarily intended for use on service 11 (Ribbleton) and introduced a dynamic new livery scheme to the company, which was to be carried by all low-floor buses. They were also the first buses in the fleet to have LED route information screens. The Scanias replaced a similar number of Lynx from the first two batches and the last of the acquired buses from Halton Borough Transport, No. 222. Nos. 211/3 were sold to members of the Malta Bus Association and were shipped from Southampton docks on

Meanwhile, the storm clouds were gathering. It became clear throughout the bitter 'bus wars' period that Stagecoach PLC had looked on Preston Bus as a prize asset to grace its ever expanding empire. Preston Bus Limited (PBL) was a compact operator with a fairly unchallenged passenger base and, although not one of the biggest operators in the county, it more than held its financial head above water. With a takeover of Preston Bus, Stagecoach would then more or less have a monopoly on the city's bus services and ensure that a rival operator, with a more aggressive appetite for expansion, could not take them over. Not surprisingly, an informal offer was made to buy the company, in July 2006, but it was met with a firm refusal. However, this did not deter Stagecoach and the company set about a strategy to undermine the incumbent's operations.

The first services introduced in direct competition to the Preston Bus services were routes 11 to Ribbleton Gamull Lane and 16 to Farringdon Park,

The first three 32-seat Optare Solos for the Orbit services arrived some ten months before they were required and were painted in the blue & ivory livery with the Preston Bus fleet name on the front only. Nos. 81/2 are seen parked in the depot yard before entering service in January 2006. They were repainted into the new low-floor bus livery just a few weeks before the start of the Orbit routes in October.

The balance of the Solo order for the Orbit routes, Nos. 84-91, all arrived in September and No. 86 was used to promote the new services in the time honoured fashion on the open flag market. It is seen on the first day of its 2-day campaign, 19th October 2006.

The company received a batch of seven Scania single-deckers with ELC 41-seat Esteem bodies in August 2006. No. 205 is seen being fitted out on the production line at the Blackburn factory only 12 days before the completed vehicle was delivered on the 17th. The first two were initially used on driver familiarisation duties but the remaining five didn't enter service until September and were consequently re-registered with '56' marks. Two of the batch, formerly Nos. 203/4, were retained by Stagecoach following the acquisition by Rotala.

Five more Scania Esteems had been ordered from East Lancs for delivery in April 2007. However, the Blackburn factory was somewhat behind with its orders and agreed to provide a number of buses on loan as a short term arrangement. The loaned vehicles all received 'Preston Bus' fleet names and fleet numbers. Dennis Dart S310 TMB (234) and Volvo B7 BX07 AZJ (235) are seen together at the Tanterton terminus. At this particular time, late summer 2007, all six buses on the route were usually loaned vehicles. The last of the five Scanias, No. 211, did not enter service until January 2008.

on 24th June 2007, both of which ran over exactly the same roads. In order to operate their Preston Citi network of routes, as they were branded by Stagecoach, a fleet of Optare Solos was drafted into their Frenchwood garage. The schedules contained an anomaly which allowed four minutes running time from the Bus Station to the first stop in Lancaster Road, a distance which could be covered in less than a minute. It was claimed that Stagecoach used this 'spare time' to hold buses in Lancaster Road and then send them forward immediately in front of the Preston Bus departures. This practice was countered by putting more buses on each route and the two operators were competing for a finite number of passengers. It was also claimed that there were irregularities in the fare structure used by Stagecoach, although this was deemed to have resulted from their introductory offer which lasted until 30th September. With the combined number of buses now following the same route to Ribbleton (service 11) amounting to at least 16 buses an hour during the day, residents on the Grange estate complained bitterly to Lancashire County Council, claiming that Grange Avenue and Fir Trees Avenue were both unsuitable for such a torrent of buses. The council responded by writing to Stagecoach and informing them of the council's concern regarding congestion and the possible damage to the road surfaces.

Preston Buses' initial response was to expand their route network beyond the city boundary, principally with the introduction of service 3 to Penwortham on 9th July, which competed directly with Stagecoach service 3. The route required the use of five Optare Solos, whilst the odd journey was sometimes covered by an Olympian or a Lynx. Eight more Solos, Nos. 77/8 and 92-7, had bolstered the fleet the previous month and these provided sufficient buses to cover the new schedules. At the same time a limited service commenced running to Southport, via Tarleton and Banks, which again shadowed the Stagecoach route. To operate this service the three remaining available Lynx, Nos. 212/8/28, were refreshed with a new coat of paint using the new fleet colours, with two of the type being required at any one time (No. 215 was also repainted but continued to be used solely on school contract work). At the end of the month Preston Bus rationalised its services and withdrew service 21 to Broadgate and services 33, 34 and 36 to Tanterton and Ingol, although the latter two districts were still adequately served by services 35 and 44.

Back in March 2007 Trident No. 192 had been the first of the type to be given a repaint in a variation of the new colours. Nos. 184/95/7/8 followed later and rather strangely each bus was painted slightly differently at the front. At the same time all of the 'route branded' Tridents had the branding removed from the sides of the vehicles. Amidst all the furore the Atlantean era came to an end, almost unnoticed, and regrettably without any form of recognition. Nos. 176/7 were both withdrawn in June and the last six, Nos. 142/3/72-5 were all taken out of service following the final day of school workings on the 20th July, but they were not officially withdrawn until August and Nos. 142/3 were the very last to be delicensed on the 29th of that month. Before disposal all except No. 172 were stored at the premises of Waltons Coaches at nearby Freckleton. Amazingly, despite their age, all six found further gainful employment. No. 142 had achieved the honour of having been the longest serving bus ever with the undertaking, having entered service on 23rd February 1980, a remarkable 27 years and 188 days of service with the same operator, which was a testament both to the bodybuilder and the standards of maintenance that were consistently achieved.

On 30th July both operators revised their services. Stagecoach introduced their new Citi routes 19 and 22, with both services following the same routes as the identically numbered Preston Bus routes. However, they differed in that buses travelling out on service 22 returned via service 19 and vice versa, thereby providing a circular route enabling passengers to travel beyond the Hospital, where the service number was changed in each direction. Unlike Preston Bus, these routes did not serve the Sharoe Green housing area or travel through the hospital grounds, but nevertheless they were introduced to target what was considered to be PBL's most profitable route corridor, along Adelphi Street and Plungington Road to Fulwood. With Stagecoach buses running to a ten minute frequency or less and Preston Bus running a near five minute frequency service, the latter two thoroughfares resounded to the sounds of more than 16 buses an hour in each direction and this did not include the buses on Stagecoach service 33 and Preston Bus service 44, which also ran through Plungington.

From the same date all of the Preston Bus journeys ran with the service number 23, irrespective of whether the bus was only going as far as the hospital or whether it was going the full distance through to Asda. Alterations were also made to services 24/5, from Lea, which were altered to run inbound via Tulketh Road instead of Pedders Lane and Egerton Road, to increase the competition with Stagecoach service 68 from Blackpool. Finally, on this date, a new service numbered 87 was introduced to serve Larches and Lea which was routed via the Railway Station and Ashton Lane Ends. This service was linked with the 14 to Fairfax Road and required six Metroriders for the combined schedule.

Four weeks later, on 26th August, Stagecoach introduced service 33 to Tanterton which followed the route of the former Preston Bus service 33 and from Ashton Lane Ends to Tanterton, ran in direct competition with the latters service 35. Meanwhile, the company had ordered five more Scania single-deckers, with East Lancashire bodywork, for delivery in April but the bodybuilder was somewhat behind with its orders and it was to be mid-September before the first of the batch, No. 208, was delivered. The remainder followed at a painfully slow rate of one bus per month. Representations were made to East Lancashire Coachbuilders who agreed to source some buses to bridge the delivery time gap. Consequently, at various times between July and November, Preston Bus had nine single deck buses on loan from a variety of owners (see Table 7) and these were used to great effect, being principally employed on services 16 and 35, thus freeing up some of their own buses which were used to supplement other services in direct competition with Stagecoach.

As the competition staged by Stagecoach gathered momentum there were claims and counter claims by both operators. In the Lancashire Evening Post, Preston Bus managing director Peter Bell was reported as saying, "We have lost customers. It is not a number we like but I would not say it is a significant threat to us. We have lost money because of all of this and our staff are worried, but this is a cash business and there is still plenty of money in the bank. I can understand people being concerned. We are employee-owned and that means our staff have invested their own money into the business, some as much as £7,500. They trust the management and know that we are all in the same boat. It is human nature. You cannot blame people for being concerned. We have tremendous customer loyalty and we have had people coming up to our staff and asking 'how are WE doing?' not 'how are you doing?'. They see us as their company and I think that sums up what we have developed here."

On the other side of the coin Stagecoach regional managing director, Chris Bowles, believed the expansion of his firm's operations in Preston was not a war. He believed it to be a multi-million pound investment and was quoted as saying "We have put £4 million into the network which we have served in one form or another for more than eight years. Our new services have brought in 40 new or nearly-new buses, generated 50 new jobs and got 33,000 people using our services every week. It shows they are popular and being used. In towns and cities up and down the country we have started new networks or expanded existing ones, often operating alongside other bus operators quite amicably. There is no reason why Preston should not also benefit in this way. The future outlook is that we will continue to seek ways to best meet our customer's needs on an on-going basis".

When later asked by the newspaper reporter, "Can we expect to see a ceasefire anytime in the near future?" Preston Bus MD Peter Bell replied: "We did not start it so we cannot finish it. We have not encouraged it. We have not done anything except compete as fairly as we can. I do not blame Stagecoach for being competitive – that is the nature of the beast – but they are a far bigger business than us with greater financial resources. The only ones who can step in to stop this are the North West Traffic Commissioner, the Office of Fair Trading or Stagecoach itself. I can see it going on for at least another 18 months." Allied to all the talk there was perceived animosity between employees of the two operators and in one famously

No.	Registration	Type	Owner	Dates in Use
Table 7				
230	PL06 TFZ	Dennis Dart, MCV Evol B40F	Northwest Bus Rentals	28/7/07 to 11/1/08
231	PL06 TGE	Dennis Dart, MCV Evol B40F	Northwest Bus Rentals	28/7/07 to 19/9/07
232	YN07 LFU	Scania OmniLink B45F	Scania, Worksop	1/8/07 to 15/10/07
233	T417 MNH	Dennis Dart, Plaxton B39F	East Lancs	10/8/07 to 9/11/07
234	S310 TMB	Dennis Dart, Plaxton B41F	East Lancs	10/8/07 to 9/11/07
235	BX07 AZJ	Volvo B7RLE, Wright B45F	Volvo Buses, Warwick	10/8/07 to 25/8/07
236	SN56 AYB	Dennis Enviro 200 B37F	Alexander, Falkirk	13/8/07 to 25/8/07
237	SK07 DYA	Dennis Enviro 300 B44F	Alexander, Falkirk	17/9/07 to 8/10/07
239	YJ57 EGU	Optare Tempo X1200 B43F	Optare, Leeds	15/11/07 to 23/11/07

The last five Leyland Atlanteans to run in service, Nos. 142/3/73-5, are seen in store at the premises of Waltons' Coaches at Freckleton in September 2007, prior to disposal by the company. No. 173 was actually bought by Waltons whilst Nos. 142/3 were snapped up by Griersons Coaches of Stockton-on-Tees; Thornes took No. 174 and No. 175 went to D D Travel at Leicester.

New in December 1999 as one of the first low-floor buses to enter the fleet for service on the Tanterton routes ELC-bodied Dennis Trident No. 193 is seen departing the Bus Station in November 2007. When new this batch of buses carried route branding for services 33 & 35; however, the branding has just been removed whilst the advert frames were fitted in the previous year. The RPH slipboard denotes a journey which was previously operated under the route number 22. Buses going to Asda carried similar slipboards with 'ASDA' in green lettering.

Only five of the Tridents, Nos. 184/92/5/7/8, were painted in the low-floor bus livery before the repainting of buses predominantly ceased after September 2008 as the company slid towards the takeover by Stagecoach. Nos. 184/92 were repainted in 2007 whilst No. 195 received the new colours in April 2008; No. 197 followed in August and No. 198 was the last to be done the following month. There were several variations to the lower front colour arrangements.

From 9th July 2007 Preston Bus commenced operation of service 2 from Preston to Southport via Longton, Tarleton and Banks and the 3 to Penwortham. The Southport service ran to a limited timetable on Mon-Sat mainly using Lynx Nos. 212/18/28, all of which were refreshed using the colours of the low-floor bus livery. Two buses were required to maintain the service and No. 218 is seen in Shore Road in Hesketh Bank on the first day of operation. Whilst the concept was well meant the intensifying competition with Stagecoach resulted in the withdrawal of the service after 3rd May 2008.

reported incident two Stagecoach drivers were alleged to have thrown eggs at Preston buses in New Hall Lane; an incident which was reported to and dealt with by the Traffic Commissioner.

In October Stagecoach made their next and final incisive moves. From Monday 7th service 16 to Farringdon Park was withdrawn and replaced by service 9, which covered the latter's route as far as the cemetery roundabout before turning left down Blackpool Road and then right into Miller Road and on to the Moor Nook estate. This was a shrewd move as the new route effectively competed with two Preston Bus services, the 16 to Farringdon Park and the 8 to Moor Nook. The final new Citi route to be introduced by Stagecoach, on 29th October, was the 32 to Savick and Larches Estate, which was intended to compete with Preston Bus services 31 (Savick) and the 88A/C (Orbit), which were the operator's principal routes to Larches. On reflection, the 32 was somewhat ill conceived and carried far fewer passengers than was hoped for and consequently it was the only service that Stagecoach withdrew before acquiring Preston Bus. The last four Scanias, Nos. 200/9-11 eventually arrived and five more Lynx, Nos. 223/4/6/7/9, were withdrawn with No. 226 following its sisters to Malta; alas, it was not to see any service on the island. Scania No. 200 gained the registration PRN 909, which had previously been carried by three other Preston buses, starting with PD3/4 No. 17, nearly 50 years before. Continuing its policy of introducing low-floor 'easy access' buses to more routes, the second batch of Scanias enabled service 16 (Farringdon Park) to benefit from the type although much later than originally planned. In November the last two Solos, Nos. 79 and 80, were received bringing the total number of the type operated to 47.

The Lancashire Evening Post carried another story on 22nd November, claiming that the 'Battling Operators' had been filming each other as the bitter 'bus wars' hotted up. This was confirmed by the PBL Company MD, who stated that the footage they had gathered may have been used as evidence in any future enquiry. To counter this statement Stagecoach also claimed to be gathering evidence. It was claimed by both sides that the footage showed some illegal practices, such as blocking bus stops. The situation was described by one reporter as "the national giants versus the established local firm, amidst an ugly backdrop of accusations, allegations of bullying, spying and egg throwing and calls for boycotts". Local Councillors also became involved, most of whom sided with the local operator, and even the city's MP, the Rt Hon Mark Hendrick, brought the issue up in Parliament accusing Stagecoach of trying to push Preston Bus off the road. Stagecoach director, Les Warneford, responded vehemently claiming that Preston Bus were conning the local residents and councillors with a "barrage of propaganda and disinformation". He also referred to the Stagecoach subsidiary as "Our local Preston Company". So by the end of the year the two operators were going head-to-head on most route corridors.

In December 2007 an informal meeting was held between the two parties when it was suggested by PBL management that the current situation was not sustainable and that both companies were losing money. Whether or not Stagecoach made an offer to buy out PBL at this meeting is not confirmed but as far as PBL was concerned the purpose of the meeting was to try and persuade Stagecoach to back off and withdraw, in order to avoid bad publicity and put an end to their losses. Finances of the company were apparently not discussed but PBL was aware that Stagecoach would have known that PBL had very little money in reserve. There is some suggestion that Stagecoach offered to sell their Preston operations to PBL, but although it was thought at the time that this was a good offer, the latter responded by saying they did not need the vehicles and there could have been staffing issues. After seeking legal advice PBL did not pursue this option.

The rivalry continued unabated throughout the following year and the situation remained unchanged for several months. Against all the odds, in March 2008, PBL again won the new tender for the Park & Ride services and obtained eight Optare Solo SRs, Nos. 1-8, to an enhanced specification to operate the services. The buses were painted in an attractive ivory, blue and magenta colour scheme and had double glazed windows, leather seats and a hard wearing imitation wooden floor. They were also powered by the new Mercedes Euro V engine. Consequently, the previous P & R buses, Nos. 59-67, were all repainted into standard fleet livery and cascaded on to normal mini-bus operated services, replacing another eight Metroriders which were sold on. At the same time the first Olympian withdrawal took place when No. 100 was sold to Northwest Bus Sales at Bolton.

When it arrived in November 2005, TPD 106X was at least more complete than it is in this view even though it had no top deck. The principal reason for its acquisition was to provide a replacement engine for A33 MRN, although many more parts were removed. Trevor Wigley's recovery truck manoeuvres the remains of the former Arriva Leyland Olympian out of the back yard into Argyll Road in December 2008.

ECW-bodied Leyland Olympian No. 133 and Leyland Lynx No. 212 are seen outside the depot just before midnight on a miserable Thursday 22nd January 2009 having performed the last rites for Preston Bus Limited, when they shadowed service bus Scania Omnidekka No. 151 on service (1)23. Most of the buses carried A4 size Window Bills during the last week proclaiming '1904-2009 Council & Employee Owned, The Last Day 22/01/09, Preston Bus'.

At the height of the 'bus wars' line ups like this one on Fishergate Bridge were not uncommon. Stagecoach Dennis Dart No. 34616 is followed by a Preston Bus Optare Solo on competing service 3 from Penwortham in September 2008. County Hall is the imposing building in the background whilst Harding's stables and horse tram depot used to stand roughly where the Stagecoach decker is waiting in the line before the railway bridge was widened by the London & North Western Railway at the beginning of the twentieth century.

A common scene at the Bus Station during the 'bus wars' sees buses queuing to leave and gain entry at the same time. Stagecoach Citi route 32, worked by Optare Solo No. 47489, was short lived and the only service which Stagecoach withdrew before the takeover. Note the figure in the hi-visibility jacket monitoring the activity in this November 2007 view.

From 30th March Stagecoach revised some of their timetables. Services on Citi route 1, between Preston and Longridge, were rationalised with the 2/2A running from Preston to Longton / Southport only. Increased frequencies were provided on Citi routes 3 and 9 at certain times of the day and certain alterations were also made to Citi routes 11, 19/22 and 33 to improve time keeping. Also at this time Citi route 32 to Savick and Larches was withdrawn. It was clear that both sides were feeling the financial pinch and Preston Bus responded with some timetable alterations of their own. Service 2 to Southport was withdrawn after 3rd May, with the last journey being worked by Lynx No. 228. In its short period of operation this service had actually attracted a cult following, presumably because of the novelty of travelling on a Lynx all the way to Southport and back. Further timetable alterations were made from the 19th, when the service number 22 was reintroduced for RPH journeys; service 87 was withdrawn and services 24/5 and 44 received minor alterations to their routes.

However, it was clear to the outsider that all was not well with the company. In early summer KPMG UK, a company specialising in, amongst other things, business support were instructed to seek potential buyers for Preston Bus and all significant UK operators barring Stagecoach were contacted. In mid-September Stagecoach contacted KPMG on behalf of Preston Bus and on 10th October an initial indicative offer was submitted to purchase the company. It seemed that there was no other operator willing to make a firm bid. One of the stumbling blocks was the company pension scheme which was complicated and had its origins buried deep in the time when the undertaking was owned and operated by the local authority. At this time, as if almost as a defiant gesture, Trident No. 198 became the last bus to be repainted into the low-floor bus livery.

Further discussions took place and at the shareholders meeting held on 29th December the Managing Director issued a statement that a firm offer had been made by Stagecoach to buy the company and that the shareholders had until 21st January 2009 to vote on the offer. Reluctantly, they had no choice and the offer was accepted. Reportedly, Stagecoach paid £6.4m for the company and acquired a fleet of 124 buses, the operating licenses, former PBL staff and the Deepdale Road premises. They also pledged to make no significant changes to the drivers and engineering staff for a period of two years but the office staff received no such assurances and many of them were subsequently made redundant.

The last day of PBL operations was Thursday 22nd January and the occasion was duly marked. Many of the buses displayed A4 size notices with black wording printed on Day-Glo yellow, proclaiming '1904-2009 Council & Employee Owned, The Last Day 22/01/09, Preston Bus'. The renowned 23.00hrs departure was witnessed by more spectators than usual and the final departure on service 123 (the last bus scheduled back into the depot) to Fulwood Asda / Longsands Lane, which was worked by Scania Omnidekka No. 151, was followed by the two oldest buses in the fleet, Olympian No. 133 and Lynx No. 212, both carrying enthusiasts and company employees past and present. The cortege wound its way through Plungington and Fulwood before it reached the Asda car park at about 23.30hrs. Here the participants disembarked to take photographs and swap vehicles. Whilst the Scania continued its journey to Longsands Lane and the depot, the special ensemble eventually returned to depot arriving at about 23.50hrs. The two buses were parked side by side at the front of the garage and as the midnight hour approached the company passed in to history – the end of an era – or so everyone thought. Over the weekend the majority of the bus fleet gained Stagecoach fleet names. Prior to the sale, two more Metroriders, Nos. 19 and 40, were disposed of. Details of the buses taken over, with their Stagecoach numbers, are shown in Table 8.

Table 8			
Type	PBL Nos.	Stagecoach Nos.	Total
Optare Solo SR	1-8	47701-8	8
Optare Metrorider	32/4-6/8/9	47912/4-6/8/9*	6
Optare Solo	51-97	47751-97	47
Leyland Olympian	101-4/6-10/2-4	14551-4/6-60/2-4	12
Leyland Olympian	123-37	14533-47	15
Scania Omnidekka	151/2	15406/7	2
Dennis Trident	182-99	18582-99	18
Scania Esteem	200-11	28510-21	12
Leyland Lynx	212/5/8/28	29212/5/8/28*	4
			124
Optare Delta T Veh. K128 UFV		26082	

*32/4/6/8 and 218 never carried their Stagecoach fleet numbers.

Whilst it was to be mid-March before all the buses had been re-numbered, Stagecoach wasted no time in implementing a repaint programme. The first bus outshopped in Stagecoach livery was Solo No. 54 (47754), on 2nd February. The programme continued at a rapid pace with some repaints taking place in the Deepdale paintshop, whilst others were sent to either Litherland at Liverpool or Carlisle to have their new colours applied. However, following a management directive at the end of March, no more buses were to be repainted and Trident No. 186 (18586), which was outshopped on 1st April, was the last. In little over two months 26 buses had been repainted (see Table 9).

Table 9		
Month	**Location**	**Buses Repainted**
February	Deepdale	47754/61/85/87
	Litherland	28510/1/3
	Carlisle	14551/7, 18587/88/93,
		47753/66/75/7
March	Deepdale	47772/94
	Litherland	28512/4
	Carlisle	14560, 15406, 18599,
		47755/64
April	Deepdale	18586

Preston Citi branding was applied to all the repainted buses at Deepdale, whilst Nos. 47785/7/94 received stylish Orbit branding. Meanwhile, all the acquired buses continued in service as before the takeover. The last six Metroriders were mainly employed on service 14 (Fairfax Road) on Monday to Friday, whilst the Lynx continued to be used in all day service on the 25 to Lea. Following the takeover the route network and vehicle scheduling needed rationalising and the appropriate notice was given to the Traffic Commissioners for changes to be implemented on 22nd March. These changes consisted of deleting the former PBL schedules on services 3 and 22; withdrawing services 24/5 and reinstating service 87. In addition the operation of services 8, 16, 19 and 22 was transferred to the Frenchwood depot, along with a number of vehicles required to operate them. The buses transferred consisted of Olympian No. 14557, Tridents Nos. 18582/3, Scanias Nos. 28512-21, Lynx No. 29228 and Solos Nos. 47759/60/2/3/5/7/96/7. At the same time some of the departure gates at the Bus Station were altered, with services 8, 11 and 16 transferred to the east side and several traditional Stagecoach and Fishwick services transferred to the west side. Not all of the former Preston buses survived the upheaval. The last of the Metroriders, Nos. 47912/5, ran for the last time on Friday 20th March, whilst Olympian Demonstrator No. 14543 and Lynx Nos. 29212/8 were withdrawn on 22nd. The Lynx and Olympian were taken to Morecambe for storage whilst the Metroriders were sent to Lillyhall.

Except for Lynx No. 29228, all the buses which had been transferred to Frenchwood were fitted with LED destination screens (excepting the Scanias and two Solos which were equipped from new), thus enabling them to be used on any services operated from that depot. The two Tridents and the Olympian could be seen working to Longridge on service 1, Southport on service 2 or to Blackpool on services 61 and 68, whilst the Lynx also made appearances on the latter service before it too was withdrawn at the end of April and taken to Lillyhall. Meanwhile, No. 29215 continued to be used on its dedicated school contract. Service 16 to Farringdon Park, which required four buses, was generally worked by a hotchpotch of vehicles; for example on 27th March the rostered vehicles consisted of Volvo B10M No. 20725, Scania No. 28512 and Solos Nos. 47774/97, somewhat of a downturn in fortunes for a route which not too long ago had benefitted from brand new low-floor Scanias. On the same day service 3 to Penwortham was covered by six Dennis Darts and transferred Solo No. 47796. Services 19/22 required an allocation of nine buses and initially the transferred Scanias were used to maintain these services.

Apart from some of the Scanias and Olympian No. 14557, all the buses transferred to Frenchwood were still in Preston Bus colours, whilst repainted buses were beginning to make their presence felt at Deepdale Road. At the same time Stagecoach buses from other depots started to appear. To cover for buses away for repaint two Solos, Nos. 47018/20, Northern Counties-bodied Olympians Nos. 13296/7 and Alexander-bodied Olympian No. 16327 were drafted in. All five buses were not considered to be in the best of mechanical health and they spent more time off the road than in use. During April and May a succession of Solos passed through the depot for various work to be carried out, including repainting. Those noted included Nos. 47003/58-61/470-3/5/7-81/3. Another notable visitor was Dennis Trident No. 19041 for repairs to minor accident damage whilst older Trident No. 18146 took root in the bodyshop after it arrived in early July, having sustained severe front end damage whilst working on service 125 to Bolton. In the ensuing months a handful of Volvo B10Ms and Dennis Darts were also noted in the depot for attention, these being Nos. 20725/898/908/18/52 and 34617/745/97. As already noted, the Farringdon Park service was being worked by a miscellany of vehicles and

Stagecoach brought three Alexander-bodied MAN single deck buses down from Scotland with the intention of using them on the Farringdon Park service. No. 22260 is seen in the dockshop being prepared for service.

ELC-bodied Scania Omnidekka No. 15406 was originally No. 151 in the Preston Bus fleet and entered service in January 2007. It is seen in Lancaster Road shortly after repainting in March 2009 but before the Preston Citi route logos have been applied. A similar painted Dennis Trident waits behind. Sister vehicle No. 152 escaped repainting into Stagecoach colours and whilst No. 151 was quickly repainted following the Rotala takeover, No. 152 wasn't done until a year later in April 2012. They were erroneously numbered 30406/7 as they should have been 40406/7 in the Rotala common fleet numbering system.

three Alexander-bodied MAN single-deckers, Nos. 22256/7/60, were transferred down from Scotland to work the service. Before being put to work they were prepared for service at Deepdale Road.

The circumstances surrounding the takeover were referred to the Office of Fair Trading (OFT), who required Stagecoach Bus Holdings Ltd to give certain assurances pursuant to Section 71 of the Enterprise Act 2002. These assurances, which were duly given on 28th February, essentially prevented Stagecoach from taking any actions which amounted to a merger of the operations of the two companies without written consent from the OFT. On the 28th May the OFT referred the takeover of PBL to the Competition Commission (CC) with the purpose of preparing a report on the circumstances surrounding and the consequences of the acquisition. Five days later the CC accepted the assurances previously given to the OFT by Stagecoach. This effectively meant that the takeover and merger was in limbo and that, amongst other things, no vehicles could be disposed of and that the Preston vehicles were to remain in their as acquired condition until such time as the matter was resolved. On 3rd September the Commission published its 'Notice of Provisional Findings' which simply stated that, "The creation of the merger situation may be expected to result in a substantial lessening of competition in the market for the provision of commercial bus services in Preston".

On 11th November the CC published its final report. The Commission had looked at the whole sequence of events and the various possible conclusions but the outcome was contained in item 21 of the summary, which simply stated, "We therefore concluded that Stagecoach should be required to divest a reconfigured PBL to a suitable purchaser within a suitable divestiture period". It also stipulated that Stagecoach should allow any new owner to establish itself for at least a 12 month period. Stagecoach appealed with regards to certain aspects of the findings but on 2nd February 2010 the CC accepted the assurances of Stagecoach with regards to the Terms of Acceptance for the divestiture of Preston Bus. PBL buses were returned from Frenchwood in dribs and drabs, with all bar the Scanias having been returned by December 2009. The three Lynx, which had latterly been in store at Lillyhall, also returned in January 2010 and were parked up in the yard off Argyll Road. Finally, the Scanias all returned en-bloc on 22nd March, almost exactly 12 months after they had left. Also that

month the Olympian Demonstrator was sold to a preservation group. No time was wasted in painting the Solos back into Preston colours and all 12 were treated to a simplified repaint (the lime green was omitted) at Deepdale, commencing with No. 47754 in February and concluding with No. 47755 at the end of May. At the same time Scania No. 28512 was similarly repainted following repairs to accident damage. It was to be a somewhat slimmed down operation which would be sold on and Stagecoach set about reducing the size of the fleet. From 15th March the former Preston routes were all reinstated, thereby reversing the alterations that Stagecoach had made 12 months earlier. At the same time the LCC contracted journeys on services 3A/B to Penwortham and New Longton, 29 to Frenchwood and service 68 to Blackpool were also taken over by Preston Bus.

The number of school contracts operated under Stagecoach had been somewhat reduced and a total of 13 more Olympians were withdrawn and sold through Ensign Bus. Former Lothian Olympian, No. 14533, had already been withdrawn at the end of February and languished in the bodyshop, stripped of its seats and various reusable parts. On 15th July six more of the type, Nos. 14534-9, left for pastures new and in September Nos. 14544-7/63/4 also left the depot. Four of the Lothians stayed local, being acquired by Walton Swift Coaches, who repainted them and used them on the very same school contracts which they had worked on when owned by Preston Bus. The other two, Nos. 14534/7, were less fortunate; having been purchased by a company in Eastleigh, they were both burnt out in a fire in March 2011. Four Solos, Nos. 47751/2/6/7, were dispersed to other members of the Stagecoach group and the stored Lynxes also passed to Ensign Bus in July.

From 7th June some alterations were made to services which included the withdrawal of routes 7 (Brookfield) and 87 (Lea/Larches). To compensate for the loss of these two routes, service 14 was re-routed away from Fairfax Road (on Mon-Sat) and altered to run via Cromwell Road to Brookfield and similarly service 31 was extended from Savick to run via Blackpool Road to Aldfield Avenue at Lea. In October the six Metroriders, which had been in store at Lillyhall, were sold to PVS at Barnsley and made the journey direct from Cumbria to Yorkshire. As the year wore on there was still no indication as to who the new buyer might be. The names of both

ELC-bodied Dennis Trident No. 18588 (40588) is seen in Friargate in March 2011 sporting the original version of the PB Rotala livery. This was the only bus painted in this fashion and it was soon altered to conform to the rest of the type. The last Trident to be repainted was No. 40586 in April 2012 and it had previously carried a pseudo 'low-floor' bus livery having been the first of the type to be hurriedly repainted out of Stagecoach livery in January 2011.

The five Plaxton-bodied Dennis Tridents acquired from Lothian Buses required a lot of work to make them roadworthy. First of the batch, No. 18540 (40540), is seen in Lancaster Road in August 2011. Ironically they replaced the last three ex-Lothian Olympians, Nos. 14540-2. However, they did not last long in the north west and were moved on to Rotala's Redditch Diamond operations in March 2013 following the arrival of the Volvo B5LH hybrids.

Table 10

Buses acquired by Rotala

Type	Stagecoach Nos.	Rotala Nos.†	Total
Optare Solo SR	47701-8	20701-8	8
Optare Solo	47761-7/9-73/6-97	20761-7/9-73/6-97	34
Leyland Olympian	14540-2*		3
Leyland Olympian	14551-4/6-60/2	42551-4/6-60/2	10
Scania Omnidekka	15406/7	30406/7	2
Dennis Trident	18582-99	40582-99	18
Scania Esteem	28510-2/5-21	30910-2/5-21	10
Leyland Lynx	29215	31215	1
			86
Optare Delta T Veh.	26082	31082	

† Rotala renumbered the fleet on 26th September 2011
* The three Lothian Olympians were withdrawn on 30/6/11.

Routes taken over by Rotala

No.	Destination	No.	Destination
1	Portway Park & Ride	23	Fulwood Asda
2	Walton-le-Dale Park & Ride	29%	Frenchwood
3A%	Penwortham	31	Lea
3B%	New Longton	35	Tanterton
8	Moor Nook	44	Ingol
14	Brookfield	68%	Blackpool
16	Farringdon Park	88A	Orbit Anti-clockwise
19/A	Royal Preston Hospital	88C	Orbit Clockwise
22	Fulwood RPH	89	Larches / Lea
% Operated under contract to Lancashire County Council			

Arriva and Go-Ahead Northern were mentioned as possibly being in the frame and even a sale to the management and employees was an outside bet. Early in the New Year an announcement was made that the company had been bought by the West Midlands based Rotala Group, for a reported £3.2m. As part of the deal Stagecoach retained some of the vehicles and a further seven Solos, Nos. 47755/8-60/8/74/5 passed to other Stagecoach Group members, and two others, Nos. 47753/4, were transferred back to Frenchwood, as were Scanias Nos. 28513/4 which were the only buses of the returnees still wearing Stagecoach colours.

On 17th January all references to Stagecoach were removed from the depot and the fleet names on the buses quickly followed, although a number of buses had already had the Stagecoach name replaced by Preston Bus. Rotala took control on Tuesday 25th January and a press release was issued immediately, the first paragraph of which read, "Rotala Plc is pleased to announce the acquisition of

Preston Bus Limited (PBL). The board considers the acquisition of the business to be a material step in the progress of Rotala and is exactly the type of acquisition we have been looking for. The enlarged group, post acquisition, will have in the region of 570 vehicles, employ 1,200 people and have an annualised turnover of about £55m". The vehicles and routes acquired were as listed in Table 10 but Stagecoach regained the operation of service 11 to Ribbleton Gamull Lane.

Just prior to the official takeover date, the first double deck vehicle to be repainted from Stagecoach colours, Trident No. 18586, had been taken into the paintshop and emerged on 26th January in the previously current low-floor bus livery, without the lime green swoops. However, Rotala had their own ideas about the fleet livery and Scania, No. 28510 (which was in Stagecoach colours), was sent to Bus & Coach World at Blackburn for a full repaint into a striking new livery of blue, silver and lime green, which was launched on 8th February. On the same date a virtually brand new Mercedes Citaro, with a 42-seat body and numbered 28522, was delivered to the depot in the same colour scheme. Scania No. 28511 followed its sister to Blackburn and returned a week later and all three buses were launched on service 16 to Farringdon Park during the month. A version of the new livery had been designed for the double deck vehicles and Trident No. 18588 was taken into the paintshop on 10th February and emerged a few weeks later in the new livery, with cream having replaced the silver. The Rotala livery incorporated large PB (Preston Bus) insignia and all vehicles soon had the wording 'Part of Rotala' added to their basic colours, on each side above the cab and entrance/exit doors. It was clear that MD Bob Dunn was not entirely happy with the front of the Trident and the next two repaints, Trident No. 18587 and Omnidekka No. 15406 returned, from having been repainted by an outside contractor at Brownhills near Walsall,

Within a month of acquiring the company Rotala placed this smart looking Mercedes Citaro into service in what was thought would be the new livery. However, although the first two repaints, Scania Esteems Nos. 28510/1 (30910/1), also received this livery all subsequent repaints were done using cream instead of silver. Although occasionally deployed on other services 10031 (28522) was generally to be found on the 16 and is seen picking up passengers in Lancaster Road in its first week of service.

In October and November 2011 the eight Optare Solo SRs were repainted into PB Rotala livery. Nos. 20701-4 were painted in the Park & Ride variation and No. 20704 is seen in Lune Street the day after arriving back from its repaint. Following a reorganisation of the Park & Ride services in March 2013 this stop was abandoned as the two routes were combined to form one through service running via Ring Way in one direction and Fishergate in the opposite direction.

In 2013 the company operated a number of services under contract to LCC. One group of such routes were the 3A, 12/A and 13/A. The 3A served Broadgate whilst the 12 ran to Longton and the 13 to Penwortham with the 'A' suffixed journeys additionally running via Broadgate. New in September 2006, Optare Solo No. 20770 was one of the 8.5 metre long buses fitted with 28 seats. It is seen on 27th April in Station Road New Longton returning to Preston. A rapid programme to repaint the Optare Solos commenced with No. 20797 in November 2011. Working back numerically the buses were taken to Wilcox of Brownhills in the West Midlands and swapped over every 4 or 5 working days with the last two being the reinstated Nos. 20762/7 at the end of June 2012.

Two of the 1992 Leyland Workington-bodied Olympians were painted in this special colour scheme for the 2012 Guild. The choice of vehicle was rather appropriate as the buses had entered service in the previous Guild Year and No. 107 (42557) had then also worn a special Guild livery for the previous Guild. Nos. 42558/9 are seen on the Market Square on 4th July for a publicity photo shoot.

with a different arrangement of the blue and green on the front which was an improvement on the first version. This revised scheme was settled on for the new Preston Bus Rotala livery (the livery came 5th in the best bus livery competition promoted by the industry publication 'Route One' in October 2012). Services 8 and 16 were both transferred back to their rightful departure gates on the west side of the Bus Station, thus grouping all of Rotala's commercial services on the same side of the concourse.

The company was still operating three of the former Lothian Olympians, Nos. 14540-2, which by then were some 23 years old. It was no surprise that they again turned towards Lothian Buses for some second hand replacements. On 20th April five redundant Plaxton-bodied Dennis Tridents, Nos. 540-4 in the Edinburgh fleet, were driven down to Lancashire, but the omens were not good as two of the buses broke down on the journey and one had to be rescued. Nos. 541/4 were in the green Park & Ride livery whilst the other three were in the standard harlequin colours. No. 544 was taken immediately to Bus & Coach World at Blackburn to be overhauled and repainted. The others followed over the ensuing weeks but ironically the first to be prepared was the last to enter service, on 29th September. They had required a considerable amount of work to make them roadworthy and all had been fitted with LED destination equipment and were given fleet numbers 18540-4. Strangely they retained the two tables in the downstairs saloon which proved to be somewhat of a novelty for the passengers. The shell of Olympian No. 14533 was sold to Trevor Wigley in April and finally left the bodyshop on the 8th. The last three runners were all withdrawn on 30th June and were sold to the York Pullman Bus Company.

Repainting of the Tridents continued at a pace, with buses being dealt with at Deepdale, Blackburn and Brownhills. At the beginning of September, No. 18583 returned from Blackburn and was the twelfth of the type to be repainted (its first repaint) and the last to have worn the original 1999 livery. At the beginning of August there were still three buses in Stagecoach livery, namely Olympians Nos. 14551/7/60. Surprisingly, No. 14551 entered the paintshop for a full repaint into the new colours and emerged on 18th August to be replaced by No. 14557. Meanwhile, No. 14560 was sent to Brownhills and returned before No. 14557 was finished, making the latter the last bus to be painted

out of Stagecoach colours and so the transformation was complete and another chapter in the history of the undertaking was closed.

On 15th September it was announced that Preston Bus had yet again been successful in retaining the contract to operate the two Park & Ride services. Keen to project its image further this was the catalyst to embark upon a rapid repainting programme for the eight Solo SRs. On 26th of the month the whole of the fleet was renumbered into Rotala's own group number series. The first of the SRs was painted at Blackburn and returned on the same date, bearing its new number 20704. The remainder were variously treated at either Blackburn or Brownhills and all had been done by the end of November. Nos. 20701-4 received new 'Park & Ride' branding for use on the Portway service. Attention then turned to the remainder of the Solos and repainting continued starting with No. 20797 and then working back numerically with all subsequent repaints being done at Brownhills.

Seven hybrid Optare Versas, Nos. 30122-8, had been on order for a few months and the first of these eventually arrived in December. Although fitted with a Mercedes Euro V engine, the function of the engine was to continually charge the 700 volt capacitors which powered the vehicles. Unfortunately, at 11.1m in length, they were too long to negotiate the Portway car park, so only three of the type received the P & R branding for use on the Walton-le-Dale service. No. 30128 was received with Black Diamond seat coverings but it returned to Yorkshire a few weeks later to have the seats changed. In July 2012 it was renumbered to 30131. The Versas initially replaced an equal number of Solos, Nos. 20761-7, five of which passed to Rotala's sister operator Black Diamond. However, Nos. 20762/7 gained a reprieve and both were repainted and later put back into service. Towards the end of December two former Stagecoach London Alexander-bodied Dennis Tridents, registration numbers X385/8 NNO, were acquired via Ensignbus for use on newly won school contract services and these eventually entered service in March as Nos. 40601/00. Some services were revised on Monday 21st May and these included some significant changes. The core frequency of the Orbit services, which had remained unchanged since they were first introduced, was extended from 15 to 20 minutes. However, the service to Larches was actually improved by introducing a full daytime

Two Dennis Tridents numbered 40600/01, with Alexander ALX400 bodies, were acquired from Ensignbus in December 2011. Originally Nos. 17321/16 in the Stagecoach London fleet they were also previously dual-doored buses. Both buses required a substantial amount of work to bring them up to an acceptable standard and it was not until the end of March 2012 that they entered service. No. 40600 is seen in Sharoe Green Lane, Fulwood on one of the two early morning 19 journeys which serve Preston College on school days and which reverted to using the service number 119 from May 2013.

As a result of the company taking on two additional routes (the 112 to Croston & 114 to Chorley) under contract to LCC three former Wrightbus Streetlite demonstrators joined the fleet in July and August 2012. Nos. 20907/9 originally had 37 seats but these were altered after a few months in service to 33; the same capacity as the shorter bodied No. 20908. No. 20909 is seen in Black Bull Lane, Fulwood in March 2013 on the long clockwise Orbit route. The Orbit routes were inaugurated on 22nd October 2006 and were in excess of 17 miles long but were contained wholly within the city boundaries and formed an integral part of the city's route network.

schedule on service 89 which strangely started from the Park & Ride stand in Lune Street and was timed to interwork with the Orbit services. In September this service was altered to run from the Bus Station. Finally, the time honoured 23.00hrs departure from the Bus Station was somewhat devalued with the final departures on only three services henceforth being so timed.

Repainting of vehicles continued at a pace. A fourth Olympian, No. 42552, was treated in May and this was followed by the remaining eight Scania Esteems, although unlike the first two Nos. 30910/1, silver gave way to the standard cream. At the same time Olympians Nos. 42558/9 were painted all-over lime green, as a base for Preston Guild 2012 proclamations. The final two Olympians, Nos. 42556/62, were repainted at the beginning of September, leaving just the Lynx as a reminder of the old order. From 22nd July the company took over the operation of service 112 to Croston and service 114 to Chorley which were operated under contract to LCC. Both services were routed via Frenchwood and replaced the 29. These required five buses to operate a combined schedule. The new vehicle requirements were covered by the two reinstated Solos and by the acquisition of three Wright-bodied Streetlites. These were former demonstrators DRZ 4018 and BRZ 9662, both 37 seaters, and CRZ 7495, a 33 seater which had latterly been used in the Olympic Torch relay as a support vehicle. They were again painted by Wilcox at Brownhills and were given the fleet numbers 20907-9. Nos. 20907/9 were down-seated to 33 a few months later. Also in July the contracted services to Penwortham were reorganised with the 3A (Broadgate), 12/A (Longton) and 13/A (Penwortham) replacing the former services 3A/B.

Investment in the fleet continued apace with the introduction of eight Wright-bodied Volvo B5LH hybrid 71-seat double-deck buses which were received in two batches of four. Nos. 40606-9 all entered service on route 23 on 7th January 2013 whilst Nos. 40619-21 joined them on the 11th April. The final vehicle, No. 40622, suffered minor bodywork damage on the ferry trip over from Ireland and although the damage was repaired fairly quickly it did not enter service until 2nd July. In a short period of time the hybrid buses have returned very impressive fuel consumption figures with savings of almost 50% over conventional diesel-engined powered buses. As a result of the acquisition of the hybrids the five former Lothian Tridents, Nos. 40540-4, left Preston for pastures new at Rotala's Redditch depot. At the beginning of March all but a handful of early morning journeys on service 19 were replaced by service 19A which did not serve Broadwood Drive and Brooklands Avenue. However, Broadwood Drive continued to be served off-peak by new route 4B which was won on tender from LCC by Preston Bus and required just one vehicle to operate it. Shortly afterwards Stagecoach made alterations to their service 4A and consequently the 4B was withdrawn after 29th June. Also from 4th March the Park & Ride services were reorganised with the two services being combined to run as route 1 from the Capitol Centre to Portway and back, via the city centre. Whilst all regular stops in Fishergate were served for buses heading to Portway, the Lune Street stop could no longer be accessed in the opposite direction and consequently Jacson Street continued to be used as the principal stop for buses travelling to the Capitol Centre.

As a member of a larger group it was inevitable that buses from other group fleets would make appearances at Deepdale. Some of Black Diamond's new hybrid Versa's were commissioned at the depot at the same time as the Preston Bus examples. Two withdrawn Tridents, Nos. 40610 (V857 HBY) and 40619 (V894 HLH) were brought up from the Midlands to provide spares whilst MANs Nos. 30801/2 and Volvo B7RLE 30859, from the Diamond fleets, have visited for attention to their engines. After a gap of nearly five years a demonstrator was taken on loan in June in the form of Alexander Dennis Enviro 200 YX62 FDG which was tried on a number of services but principally service 35 to Tanterton. At the end of August Scania No. 30912 was sold to Volvo Bus & Coach at Coventry thereby reducing the fleet by one to 98. Solo No. 20791 was involved in a fatal accident on Sunday 22nd September when it was in collision with a stolen car on Larches Lane whilst working on service 89.

In November a further contract was won from LCC to operate service 75 which had been operated by Cumfy Bus and ran daily from Preston to Blackpool via Kirkham and Poulton-le-Fylde. The buses acquired to operate the service consisted of four slimline 28-seat Optare Solos which were surplus to requirements in the Rotala Diamond fleet. Numbered 20004/11 and 20810/1 they were repainted at Brownhills and prepared for service at Deepdale Road. Only No. 20810 was fitted with a farebox as it was intended that the other three would be used solely on the 75 which they duly took over on 9th December.

To court controversy it was announced in December 2012 that the Council intended to demolish the iconic Bus Station citing that, in the prevailing economic climate, the city could no longer afford to adequately maintain such a mammoth structure. However, in the ensuing twelve months the Bus Station gained a reprieve as it was granted listed building status which should grant access to other sources of funding and so it remains to be seen what alterations and improvements will be made. Also of major significance was the announcement by PB Rotala MD Bob Dunn that the company was looking to relocate the depot away from its present site in Deepdale Road and that plans to occupy a new site within the city were actively being pursued. After looking at several green field sites on which to build new facilities the company has identified existing premises in Greenbank Street, which are sited within a mile of the city centre, as a possible option. Formerly owned by Goss, the world renowned makers of printing presses, most of the site was vacated in 2006 leaving the main assembly building empty. Erected in 1958 this building has been deemed suitable for conversion to a bus garage and with a substantial amount of adjacent open land (which used to be occupied by Greenbank railway sidings) there is ample room to house the fleet and provide all the necessary maintenance and cleaning facilities. At the time of writing the move was still at the planning stage but nothing is likely to be finalised until redevelopment planning issues concerning the existing site have been resolved.

On a rather sad note Depot Engineer Jim Hilton, who had only recently been appointed as Rotala Group Engineer, died suddenly of a heart attack whilst on company business in Manchester on 21st August. As a mark of respect Volvo No. 40606 was adorned with the name "In memory of Jim Hilton 1947-2013" which it carried on the front offside corner.

In the early hours of Friday 20th December a large hole appeared in the depot access road which crosses the 'Moor' and enables buses to access the garage by the rear entrance. It was suspected that the collapse may have been linked to the presence of Moorbrook culvert which lies approximately 9 metres below the access road in the locality of the collapse. Besides the actual collapse there are other signs of possible nearby ground movement. It was therefore clear that some major investigative work would be required which at the time of writing had not yet commenced. The affect of the collapse has meant that buses can now only access the depot from the front of No. 2 garage as well as exiting through the same entrance. Consequently, not only has parking access been reduced on the 'Moor', but parking space has also been reduced inside the garage itself so as to enable the movement of vehicles. Consequently, a number of buses, amounting to as many as 15 on occasions, have been outstationed at the Capitol Centre Park & Ride site and these were being used to maintain the school contract services from this location. It was not known how long this situation was likely to continue but it could be for quite some time whilst the cause of the collapse was ascertained and what could turn out to be quite substantial repairs carried out.

So, to sum up the first three years of Rotala's tenure: the fleet size has been increased by in the region of 17% and 15% of the buses operated are hybrids. All the vehicles (except the Lynx) now wear a uniform livery and are smartly turned out, reversing the trend which was created during the years of ownership uncertainty. The core city route network has been maintained and additional tendered routes have been won which take Preston buses out to neighbouring towns. Significant computer technology has been introduced with the fitting of new intelligent ticket issuing machines to the whole fleet and the additional fitting of devices to the buses which monitor the performance of the driver with regards to fuel consumption, etc. One thing is certain and that is that further challenges will lie ahead but it would appear that in Rotala there is leadership to meet these challenges head on and continue to provide a quality transport service for the citizens of Preston.

5. Liveries and Destination Equipment

Liveries

1904. One early document describes the colours of the new trams as being 'peony and yellow' whilst another source reports the colours as being 'crimson and cream'. Unfortunately, the official description of the Preston Corporation Tramways does not give any detail of their outward appearance but it does however describe the inside of the saloons as being made chiefly of oak with the ceiling being of bird's eye maple, decorated with side panels of green and gold. Whatever their initial outward appearance the livery could probably have also been described as being maroon and deep cream and although the latter took on paler shades over the years these two colours predominated until 1966.

The trams were fully lined out along the sides and at each end. The town crest, showing a lamb and the letters 'PP', for Proud Preston, was positioned on the sides in the centre of the tram, with the inscription '**PRESTON CORPORATION TRAMWAYS**' in large gold letters underneath. Gold shaded fleet numbers, at either end, completed the attractive layout. The Corporation Tramways lettering was later dropped. The first buses, the Leyland G7s, also had large gold lettering on the sides which simply read '**PRESTON CORPORATION**'. The SG7s and A13s, which followed, had small lettering low down at the front of the sides, which again proclaimed 'Preston Corporation Tramways'.

1926. With the acquisition of the three Leviathans a new livery arrangement was adopted. These buses had three cream bands, cream window surrounds and a white roof. The remainder of the vehicle was painted maroon and they were fully lined out with large gold shaded fleet numbers.

1933. With the introduction of TD3s, Nos. 54-9 in November, the layout was changed. The window surrounds were now maroon and the front and rear roof domes were also maroon. The cream was now applied in three bands, one below both deck windows and in a wider band at the cantrail. The roof was still white between the domes. Lining out and gold shaded fleet numbers continued to be applied. The exact original livery of the pre-war single deck buses, Nos. 79-82, is not known but photographs of No. 83, taken when the bus was new in December 1937, seem to show that although

the body panels were clearly maroon, the window surrounds and waistrail were clearly painted in a lighter colour – was this yellow or deep cream? The pre-war buses were always well turned out and normally looked immaculate. However the war years took their toll and the fleet looked decidedly down at heel at the end of the war.

1935. All of the batch of TD4cs, Nos. 11-32, and the two Lion LT7cs, Nos. 81/2, were used as an experiment to trial different makes of paint. Nobels Dulux paint was used on No. 11; Dockers Syntholux paint was used on Nos. 12/5-20/2-4/6/7/9-32, 81/2; British Anti-fouling paint was used on No. 13; Leyland's Synthetic paint was used on No. 14 and Kearsley's paint was used on Nos. 21/5/8.

1946. The first of the PD1s, delivered in July, helped to smarten up the appearance of the fleet. The predominant colour was still maroon and the three cream bands were painted in a similar fashion to the pre-war Titans. The buses were no longer lined out and although the fleet numbers were still gold, they were of a much smaller size. All the PD1s wore this livery when new. Later repaints omitted the cream band below the upper deck windows. Inside, the saloons were painted dark green from just above the floor levels to the underside of the windows; the section from below to above the window line was painted a light green and the saloon ceilings were white. These colours were used until the change to blue and ivory at the end of 1966.

1950. In December the first of many PD2s entered the fleet. The batch of PD2/1s, Nos. 108-27, were painted differently to the PD1s. The cream was now applied to the cantrail and both upper and lower deck window surrounds. This batch of buses appears to have been unique in wearing this livery arrangement.

1952. In March the first buses of a batch of ten PD2/10s were delivered and these were again painted differently, whereby only the section from the cantrail to below the lower deck windows was painted cream. This arrangement was adopted for the two subsequent batches of PD2/10s and for subsequent PD1 and TD repaints until 1956.

1956. With the delivery of the first Crossley-bodied PD2/10 in July, an even more simplified livery was introduced, whereby the cream was now only applied in a wide band at cantrail level which thinned out considerably above the cab and across the front of the vehicle. This was adopted as the standard livery for the next ten years and all of

1904 4-wheel car No. 10, which was built at the town's Strand Road Works, waits outside the Bull & Royal Hotel at the top of Church Street with a service for Ribbleton. In this view No. 10 has subsequently received a Top Cover with all but three of the type receiving this modification.

Number 44 was an English Electric-bodied Leyland TD2 and was one of a batch of ten buses bought in July 1932 to replace the trams on the Farringdon Park and Penwortham routes, which were the first services to be converted to motorbus operation. This particular bus was re-bodied at the same factory less than eight years later.

the PD1s, PD2s and PD3s (except Rebuild No. 59) eventually wore this arrangement. It is thought that only three TDs were so painted viz. Nos. 34, 40 and 58. With the livery arrangement having changed three times in only six years it was a number of years before standardisation was achieved.

1966. The Transport Committee decided it was time for a radical change. They may have been influenced by the visit of Kingston-upon-Hull Transport Leyland Panther No. 173, in August, or it may have been that the consensus of opinion was that the town's colours were already blue and white – after all Preston North End's kit colours were just that. Whatever the reason, the General Manager was asked to paint one of the undertaking's buses in blue and white. Consequently, PD2/10 No. 43 was painted Oxford Blue and broken white and was inspected by members of the Committee on 22nd September. Members of the Town Council were also given the opportunity to inspect the bus when it was parked outside the Municipal Buildings (Town Hall) in Lancaster Road on 28th September and No. 43 re-entered service the following day. Three further buses, Nos. 33/5 and 81 (see Table 11) were then painted in different colour schemes and the good citizens of Preston were also invited to comment on the four buses, as they were used on most of the town's stage services. It was eventually resolved at the committee meeting held on 12th December to adopt a new livery of middle blue and ivory in the arrangement worn by No. 35. The livery also incorporated three thin black lines; below the upper deck windows and above and below the lower deck windows. Fleet numbers were still gold and the town's crest adorned each side. The insides of the saloons were now painted blue and white. Five of the Crossleys were never painted blue and ivory, viz. Nos. 25-8, 30, whilst only five of the PD2/1s, viz. Nos. 122-6 were done. All the PD3s were painted thus but as the last few PD1s only survived into 1968, none were so painted although surprisingly both the PS1s were.

1968. Following the introduction of the first Panthers, in December, each subsequent batch wore a slightly different livery arrangement when new. The arrangement worn by the last batch of new Panthers, Nos. 230-6 (RTF 430-6L), was adopted as the standard and all subsequent single deck buses, including mini-buses, wore this livery. Originally, Panthers Nos. 201-4 had larger gold numbers than the rest when new. The last bus in these colours was Metrorider No. 35 (the first being PD2/10 No. 35) which was repainted into the subsequent new livery in January 2005.

1973. In November PD3 Rebuild No. 5 was outshopped in a radically different arrangement of the same colours. The blue was applied to the roof, upper deck window surrounds, cantrail band and skirt; the remainder was ivory. All the PD3s eventually wore this arrangement as did all the Atlanteans and new Olympians.

1974. Following Local Government re-organisation on 1st April, for the first time since the trams and early buses, a fleet name was applied to the sides of the buses, namely '**Borough of PRESTON**', which still incorporated the town crest. Originally this was applied to the sides below the lower deck windows but on double-deckers, from September 1981, it was later repositioned on the sides at the front between decks. By November 1977 all the vehicles in the fleet carried the name.

1983. Atlanteans Nos. 1 and 2 and Olympian No. 3 were painted in a non-standard livery which consisted of ivory with a mid-blue skirt and three blue bands of different shades, at cantrail level. Additionally, the two Atlanteans had black window surrounds and black fleet numbers. The fleet name simply read '**PRESTON**' in large black outline letters with no town crest. All three were painted into the standard livery in 1990. In 1988 six of the Renault mini-buses, Nos. 47-9 and 75-7, had similar black outline names on their bonnets.

1985. From July the fleet numbers were changed from the gold numerals to smaller silver numerals, similar to those used at the time by the National Bus Company fleets. This was a gradual process which was first applied to Atlantean No. 166, and was only done as the buses were repainted.

1986. Four Leyland Nationals, Nos. 5-8, were acquired from the Merseyside Passenger Transport Executive in August and these ran for two years in their 'as acquired' livery of verona green and jonquil, with a brown skirt. They also had black window surrounds and '**Borough of PRESTON**' fleet names were applied. In 1988, the three survivors were painted into the standard livery with '**PRESTON BUS**' fleet names.

Table 11	
Crossley-bodied PD2/10 No. 33	Ivory with light blue window surrounds and roof.
Crossley-bodied PD2/10 No. 35	Mid-blue with ivory window surrounds and cantrail band.
Leyland-bodied PD2/10 No. 43	Mainly Oxford blue with broken white between decks.
MCW-bodied PD2/10 No. 81	Mainly light blue with ivory between decks.

Leyland TD4 No. 12 is wearing a hybrid version of the three cream bands livery whereby the top band has been omitted. Only a handful of TDs and PD1s ever carried this abridged version. No. 12 was one of four all-metal Leyland-bodied machines received for the last tramway conversion in December 1935 and is seen on the Ashton Lane Ends C stand in Harris Street. This bus was withdrawn in November 1954 and sold to Progress Motors of nearby Chorley.

Virtually brand new 1950 Leyland PD2/1 No. 117, with lowbridge PD1A No. 105 behind, wait outside North End's Deepdale ground in Hollins Road for a First Division match to finish circa 1951. Note the use of the letter 'O' for Other service. No. 117 lasted until April 1970 when it was replaced by the second batch of Marshall-bodied Leyland Panthers. The stand behind the buses was the old Spion Kop which was demolished in 1998 and replaced by the new 6,000 seater Bill Shankly Kop.

Fairly new 1952 Leyland PD2/10 No. 45 is seen passing between the Cenotaph and the Market Square in July 1953, before turning on to its stand in Birley Street, in front of the photographer's vantage point. A few weeks later the PL was linked with the FP service. This batch of PD2s were the first buses to be painted in this fashion, whereby the cream was applied to the cantrail and lower deck window surrounds only. This version was superseded by the simple single cream band from 1956. The Cenotaph was originally erected to commemorate those who lost their lives in WW1 and was dedicated in June 1926.

New in 1933, Leyland TD3s Nos. 56 and 58 were both re-bodied by Croft in 1945 and are seen in Deepdale Road on Football Specials returning to Town after a match, circa 1957. No. 58 has the simplified 1956 livery of a single cream band and was withdrawn in October 1957 whilst No. 56 was withdrawn in the preceding month. It is thought that only two other pre-war Titans, Nos. 34 and 40, received the simplified single cream band livery. The landmark County (Arms) Hotel was demolished in 2007.

The Corporation operated a total of 18 Leyland PD2/10s fitted with Park Royal designed Crossley built bodywork, which entered service between July 1956 and December 1957. No. 33 was one of the four buses trialled for the new blue and ivory livery, in September 1966, and is seen alongside the impressive Miller Arcade in Birley Street in its unique colour scheme.

Number 81 was one of a batch of five MCW-bodied Leyland PD2/10s which entered service on 1st November 1955. Also seen alongside Miller Arcade in Birley Street, circa 1967, it was one of the four PD2/10s which were painted in experimental liveries in September 1966. The imposing shopping Arcade was opened in 1899.

1987. New Leyland Tiger coach, No. 40, was received in a different version of the livery worn by Nos. 1-3, although additionally the roof was painted blue. It also had '**PRESTON COACH**' fleet names. Dodge / Renault mini-buses were received with '**PRESTON MINI**' fleet names, whilst the larger buses henceforth carried '**PRESTON BUS**' fleet names. The Atlanteans also received one of four slogans at the front which read either '*Your Friendly Service*', '*We Care*', '*For Easy Shopping*' or '*The Best Bus in Town*'. The Dodge / Renault mini-buses had black fleet numbers in the style of the similar Greater Manchester Transport vehicles.

1991. Acquired East Lancs-bodied Dodge mini-bus No. 6 was painted all white, for operation on the Portway Park & Ride service. In November 1992 it was repainted blue and ivory with Riversway 'Park & Ride' lettering.

1994. Metroriders Nos. 1-4 were received in November with 'PARK & RIDE' lettering on the front, sides and back for the Portway service. In 1998 Nos. 3 and 4 were replaced by Nos. 39 and 40, which were also so adorned. Nos. 8-10, of the same batch, were used from new in March 1995 for approximately one month painted all ivory, before the blue was added at Deepdale.

1996. A number of Atlanteans, and two Olympians, were outshopped between November 1996 and February 1999 with the addition of four thin black lines, one at each interface of the blue and ivory. The vehicles so treated were Nos. 104/6/42/3/8/52/6-9/62/3/6/7/70-2/4/5.

1997. At the end of the year Renault mini-bus No. 92 was painted using the standard arrangement of the colours but using a different shade of blue, known as Tahiti Blue. It was withdrawn still in these colours, following an accident in October 1999.

1999. In March, Olympian No. 107 was used to try out different colours for a completely new livery scheme. A lighter blue was applied to the roof and upper deck window surrounds and to the lower deck panels below the windows, with a dark blue skirt. The area in between was successively painted in different shades of yellow or cream before a cream shade was eventually decided on. The fleet numbers reverted to larger numerals in black. At the same time Olympian No. 106 was painted in the lighter blue but with a deeper shade of cream. However, the final colours, as applied to No. 107, were adopted as the standard livery until September 2006. All the Olympians, Lynx and Metroriders eventually wore these colours,

although the layouts differed on the different types of vehicle. Solos Nos. 51-8 and 81-3 were the only ones of the type to be delivered in these colours and rather surprisingly even a number of Atlanteans were treated, viz. Nos. 142/3/52/8/9/65/8/70/2-7, although the livery worn by No. 176 was a special variation.

In June, Olympian No. 110 was outshopped in a different arrangement of this livery. The lighter blue was applied in swoops, on the upper deck from the back and on the lower deck towards the front. The section in-between the swoops was cream. A dark blue was applied to the skirt and 'PRESTON BUS' fleet names, with the town crest, adorned the sides, front and back. Additionally, the side fleet names had the inscription 'Your local service' underneath. This was done to try out a new colour scheme for the impending new Dennis Tridents.

The livery arrangement was only changed slightly for the Tridents, in that the lower blue swoop only came part way up the cab at the front and not to the top of the cab, as on No. 110. '**PRESTON BUS**' fleet names were applied in cream on the front and in blue on the sides, at the front in between decks. Most of the Tridents and the first Solos were also route branded under the umbrella of 'Super Routes'. Route branding was removed in 2007, with the Solos receiving a full repaint into the then new low-floor bus livery.

2001. Metrorider No. 30 was painted in an experimental version of the blue and cream livery with an additional wide blue swoop at the back. No others of the type were done and the swoop was painted out in April 2004.

2002. In November, Solos Nos. 59-67 were received in a special livery of lilac and light blue with a dark blue skirt, for use on the Park & Rides services. They also had appropriate lettering for the services. They were repainted into the new standard low-floor bus livery in 2008.

2003. In February Volvo B10M coach, T894 HBF, was acquired from Bassett Coachways, painted in a mixture of turquoise and light grey and it remained in these colours during its three and a half year stay with the undertaking.

2006. With the delivery of the first Scania Esteems in August and a new batch of Solos, starting with No. 68 in September, the livery was changed to one of light blue and cream with a lime green swirl on the side and flashes on the back. Fleet numbers were now lime green. Eventually, all the Solos wore this livery. Five Tridents were treated

Following the reorganisation of bus services in November 1980, the Lane Ends C was replaced by service 33 which was an extension to the new housing development at Tanterton. 1976 East Lancs-bodied Leyland Atlantean No. 114 is seen in Woodplumpton Road leaving Lane Ends behind in July 1983. No. 114 was withdrawn in November 1990 when it passed to the Yorkshire operator Sheffield Omnibus who eventually took 26 former Preston Atlanteans.

The last batch of Atlanteans was received in 1983 and the last two had bodywork built by ELC with 74 high back seats and a single doorway. Originally to have been numbered 178/9 they were actually numbered 1 and 2 although they were renumbered into the common sequence in later years. No. 2 is seen on display on the Market Square on 14th June 1983.

Three ELC-bodied Dodge mini-buses and a Reeve Burgess-bodied example were acquired to operate the newly won contract for the Portway Park & Ride service in January 1991. No. 6, which is carrying a unique 'Park & Ride' colour scheme, was one of three of the type which started life with Barrow Borough Transport. It is seen at the original picking up point in Fishergate in September 1993.

Nine lilac and blue painted Solos with air conditioning and double-glazed windows were introduced to the two Park & Ride services in December 2002. No. 62 is seen waiting for passengers in Jacson Street in November 2005. They were replaced on the Park & Ride services in May 2008 by Solo SRs Nos. 1-8 and were then repainted for ordinary stage work. Nos. 59-61 were retained by Stagecoach in January 2011 whilst Nos. 63-6 passed to Rotala's subsidiary operator Black Diamond in February 2012, following the entry into service of the new Optare Versa hybrid buses.

to a double deck version, viz. Nos. 184/92/5/7/8 and the two Omnidekkas, Nos. 151/2, were also painted likewise. In 2007 the four remaining Lynx, Nos. 212/5/8/28, were painted in a simpler version of the livery with no swoops. Several Solos, Trident No. 186 and Scania No. 202 were painted out of Stagecoach colours in 2010 into a simplified version of this livery which omitted the green.

2008. Optare Solo SRs Nos. 1-8 were painted blue and white with magenta swirls for the new Park & Ride contract. Appropriate lettering, in blue and lilac, completed the colour scheme. These were the last new buses delivered to the erstwhile Preston Bus Ltd. The last bus repainted in Preston colours was Trident No. 198 in September 2008.

2009. Following the takeover by Stagecoach, in January, a programme of repainting buses in Stagecoach colours was rapidly implemented. This is detailed in Chapter Four.

2011. A new Rotala Preston Bus livery of cream, lime green and two shades of blue was introduced in March starting with Trident No. 18588 (40588). Following some minor modifications to the layout the colours were applied to the whole fleet, except Lynx No. 31215, with the last bus so treated being Olympian No. 42556 in September 2012. Fleet numbers were applied in either white or grey depending on the type of vehicle. Solo SRs Nos. 20701-4 and Optare Versas Nos. 30123-5 carried a Park & Ride version of the standard livery. Apart from some of the early repaints the majority of the work was contracted out to Wilcox of Brownhills in the West Midlands.

Special Colour Schemes

Only a handful of special colour schemes have adorned Preston's buses and trams over the years and these are detailed below :-

ER & TCW 1904 4-wheel cars

One source states that three cars were decorated for the coronation of King George V, in June 1911, and that three cars were also decorated for the Royal visit to Preston in July 1913. It has not been possible to determine how many cars were used for each occasion although various photographs show a number of 4-wheel cars suitably decorated.

ER & TCW 1904 bogie car No. 30

For the 1922 Guild this car was adorned with light bulbs and was displayed as an illuminated car

at night. For this purpose the seats and handrails on the upper deck were removed and a large illuminated version of the town crest was affixed to the front of the roof at one end. The large crest was subsequently used on Leyland Tiger No. 80 and is still in existence, being presently mounted above the depot entrance.

English Electric-bodied Tiger No. 80

In 1950, National Child Safety Week, which ran from 19th to 25th March, concentrated on portraying the message of the importance of safety on the country's roads. Leyland Tiger No. 80 was used as an elaborate display to portray this message. Painted all white, the windows were covered over on the sides and back and various road safety messages were displayed using light bulbs which could be illuminated at night, to great effect. No. 80 was presumably restored to its previous condition as a service bus as it was not withdrawn until March 1954.

Seddon-bodied Panther No. 236

In 1982 Lancashire County Council launched a countywide ticket initiative, marketed as the Red Rose Rambler (RRR), and to promote the ticket buses from a number of Lancashire fleets were painted into a distinctive advertising scheme, which incorporated the Red Rose. Preston was the only fleet to use a single deck bus and Panther No. 236 entered service on 18th October so adorned. On 28th March of the following year all the promotional buses were gathered on Preston's Market Square at a publicity event. Whilst in these colours No. 236 underwent a fleet renumbering to simply 36, but the new number was never actually carried as it was withdrawn on 21st August 1984, still in the RRR colours.

ECW-bodied Olympian No. 3

Before taking up normal stage service duties with the undertaking, Olympian No. 3 was used by Leyland Vehicles as a demonstrator and as such visited many bus operators throughout the UK. For this purpose it carried the lettering 'OLYMPIAN DEMONSTRATOR – Leyland Bus' in between decks, on both sides. The lettering was the only variation from the three blue bands fleet livery and was removed in November 1985, when it was replaced by the black outline 'PRESTON' name.

Leyland Tiger TS4 No. 80 was decorated for Child Safety week in March 1950. The slogans are formed of light bulbs which carried the message clearly in the dark. The crest above the cab could also be illuminated and is the same crest which was fitted to one of the bogie cars for the 1922 Guild and which presently sits above the main entrance to the depot.

The undertaking bought two batches of Seddon Pennine-bodied Leyland Panthers each consisting of seven vehicles. Nos. 223-9 entered service in the spring of 1971 whilst Nos. 230-6 followed just over a year later, except for No. 236 which was fitted with experimental CAV Transmission and was used as a demonstrator until April 1973 when it finally entered normal service. It did, however, take part in the 1972 Guild Trades Procession. In this May 1984 view No. 236 is seen in Tulketh Brow, Ashton heading back to town. It was one of the last three Panthers in service and was withdrawn only a few months later and sold to the Isle of Man National Transport.

Leyland-bodied Olympian No. 107

One of a batch of eight new Olympians which joined the fleet in the 1992 'Guild' year, No. 107 was chosen to advertise the forthcoming year-long events spectacular. The bus was completed by Leyland in October 1991 and was exhibited at the Bus & Coach Exhibition in Birmingham on the 14th. However, it didn't enter service with Preston until 5th February 1992. No. 107 wore the basic fleet livery of blue and cream, but had additional lettering for the Guild in-between decks on the sides; it also had two town crests on the front, one on each side of the destination box, a peculiarity which was not only confined to No. 107 but which was also applied to some of the other Olympians. No. 107 retained this look until January 1993.

East Lancs-bodied Atlantean No. 176

In September 1998 No. 176 was turned out, superbly painted, in the original immediate post-war livery of maroon with three cream bands. In order to make the layout look as authentic as possible, prior to painting, it received considerable work to the body panels and mouldings were applied to accommodate each of the cream bands. Gold lettering was applied to the front of the vehicle proclaiming '1879 PRESTON BUS 1999' and 'Celebrating 120 years of Preston's bus and tram services'. To complete the effect, original style tram numerals were used for the fleet numbers. No. 176 remained in this colour scheme until March 2004, when it was painted into another commemorative layout using the normal fleet colours but with the blue applied to the whole of the vehicle other than the three bands, which were painted deep cream. This was done to celebrate 100 years of bus and tram operation by Preston Bus and its predecessors, and appropriate lettering was applied to proclaim the event. No. 176 was withdrawn in this guise on 4th June 2007.

Leyland-bodied Olympians No. 42558/9 (108/9)

Two of the 1992 Olympians were repainted in June 2012 in all-over lime green with Guild 2012 lettering in white and yellow.

Advert Colour Schemes

Other than the treatment of MCW-bodied PD3A/1 No. 88, to commemorate the 1972 Preston Guild, all-over advert colour schemes only really came to prominence at the end of the 1970s. Throughout the 1980s and 1990s a number of Atlanteans, Olympians and mini-buses were subjected to this treatment. Some of the earlier schemes were quite colourful, particularly the Hitchens Kitchens and Harlequin Chocolate schemes which adorned Atlanteans Nos. 128 and 160 respectively. Whilst the former was local to the town, the latter also appeared on buses belonging to other undertakings. Atlantean No. 177 had the distinction of carrying three different adverts whilst Olympian No.(1)37 also managed two. Most of the advert schemes were painted on to the vehicle and, nearly always, the base colour was applied at the Deepdale Road depot, with the finishing work done by an outside contractor or signwriter. Whilst the only full size bus advert applied with stick-on vinyls was that to Lynx No. 229, the Metrorider and Solo rear adverts were all stick-on vinyls.

Destination Equipment

Originally, the 1904 cars had a destination box mounted on two metal poles at each end of the upper deck which contained a roller blind showing the destinations only. All but three of the first 26 open top cars had received Top Covers by 1913; at this time they would also appear to have been fitted with side destination boxes, behind the centre window of the lower deck. The three 1912 United Electric Company cars, Nos. 31-3, had front and side destination boxes as did the six double deck cars, Nos. 34-9, which were new two years later. These latter cars also had a separate route letter display, above each cab, and this may have been the first use of letters to identify a particular route. Later, the front destination boxes were removed from most trams and they continued to display the route letter only. All the reconstructed trams were only built with route letter boxes at their ends and destination boxes on the sides.

Destinations known to have been used on the trams are as follows, but they are not necessarily in the order in which they appeared on the blinds :- FULWOOD via North Road, MOOR PARK, WITHY TREES, SHAROE GREEN, FULWOOD BARRACKS via North Road, DEEPDALE STATION, LANCASTER ROAD, DEPOT

1983 East Lancs-bodied Leyland Atlantean No. 176 is depicted in Longridge Road, Ribbleton wearing the first of its two commemorative liveries. It was painted in the immediate post war livery of maroon with three cream bands in September 1998 just prior to performing a star role in the depot open day activities. This was then changed to blue with three cream bands in March 2004 to celebrate 100 years of bus and tram operation by the company. It was one of the last handful of Atlanteans to be withdrawn in the summer of 2007.

In this October 1984 view three East Lancs-bodied Leyland Atlanteans are seen on the 'Moor' displaying their all-over advert colour schemes. No. 172 carried the Lion Bitter advert from new in November 1982; No. 160 carried the Terry's Harlequin chocolates advert for just over a year and No. 128 invited you to buy a Hitchens' Kitchen for the same period of time. It was unusual to have three buses in advert colours at the same time. The depot engineer at the time, George Orme, kindly arranged for this line-up.

Leyland PD1A No. 93 was new in 1947 and is painted in the 1952 livery variation. Already the bus has been modified at the front and now only has a single destination aperture which is only just wide enough to display the destination. No route letters are included on the blind. It is seen in front of the Harris Library in Birley Street.

A bleak mid-winter scene sees East Lancs-bodied Atlantean No. 134 at the erstwhile Longsands Lane (originally denoted as Long Sand Lane) terminus on 11th February 1981. All the Atlanteans carried this livery for most of their working lives until 2004 when the remaining 14 examples were painted into the 1999 livery. No. 134 entered service in January 1979 and was initially used as a demonstrator. It was disposed of to Sheffield Omnibus in July 1992. Always an infrequent service with only a handful of daily departures, buses first started running to this country outpost in May 1938. The service was withdrawn after 12th July 1987 and the area is now unrecognisable, being the location of J31A on the M6 motorway.

ONLY, FOOTBALL GROUND, FULWOOD, PENWORTHAM, PENWORTHAM BRIDGE, STRAND ROAD, FISHERGATE HILL, CENTRAL STATION, SKEFFINGTON ROAD, CEMETERY, FARRINGDON PARK, OLD ENGLAND, RIBBLETON, POWIS ROAD, ASHTON and SPECIAL CAR.

This list is by no means exhaustive but no records now exist of what was contained on the tram blinds. Of particular interest is the insert 'DEEPDALE STATION' which was situated on the branch line from Preston's Central Station to Longridge, and was adjacent to the underbridge on Deepdale Road, only a 100 yards or so from the depot. The station closed when the line was closed to passenger services on 31st May 1930. POWIS ROAD was a turn back point on the Ashton route as was OLD ENGLAND on the Ribbleton route, whilst trams could turn back at both SKEFFINGTON ROAD and the CEMETERY on the Farringdon Park route. The insertion of STRAND ROAD is somewhat unusual as none of the tram routes directly served this thoroughfare but it was of course where the Works, which built most of them, was situated.

The first motorbuses, the Leyland G7s, had a front and side destination box, but no route letter display. Subsequent batches of the early single-deckers simply had the front destination box. The first buses to be delivered new, with a separate route letter box, were the English Electric-bodied Leyland TD2s and Lions, which were received in June and July 1932. The 1928-built Lions later had a route letter box attached under the roof, above the bonnet, which wasn't in keeping with the front end appearance of the vehicle, as it was much deeper than the destination aperture. The TD2s had the route letter box above the destination box at the front, whilst on the single-deckers it was on the nearside of the vehicle. Both types had side destination boxes and the double-deckers also had a rear destination box but these were gradually removed after the war. The PD1s were the first new double-deckers to have the front destination and route letter boxes side by side. Many pre-war TDs were similarly altered in the 1950s as they were overhauled. All the PD2s were received with separate destination and route letter apertures but, from the introduction of the first PD3s in January 1959, a single screen aperture was introduced which displayed a single blind with the destinations and route letters side by side. A number of TDs and PD1s were similarly modified but could

only show the destinations, whilst all of the MCWs and some of the Crossley-bodied PD2s were also treated and these were fitted with blinds that had the route letters next to the destinations.

From the introduction of the trams, linen blinds showing white letters on a black background had always been used. The display of numbers had always been impossible as no number blind displays were included on the blinds. With the introduction of the first Panthers, in December 1968, separate number/letter and destination apertures were provided at the front on the MCW-bodied batch, although the numbers were now on the offside. The number/letter aperture did at least include two separate rolls so that the 'F' and the 'P' for Farringdon Park could be put up separately and theoretically any combination of two letters could now be displayed. Also included were the numbers 0 to 9, most of which were required to be shown on the jointly operated services, eg. P4. All subsequent batches of Panthers had a single aperture containing two letter/number blinds and a destination and they all had side destination displays at roof level, behind the entrance doors. The Atlanteans continued this trend and all but the last two had the same front and side arrangements. Nos. 1 and 2 originally had a destination box at the side, as opposed to a built in aperture, but the boxes were later removed and not replaced whilst Nos. 172-7 had their side destination apertures plated over at the end of 2005.

The three Bristol mini-buses had just a front screen with two letter/number rollers and a destination roller. The Dodge mini-buses had a three number and destination box behind their windscreens, whilst the later Renaults had a similar appearance to the earlier Bristols, where the screens were built into the vehicles. The next generation of mini-buses, the Metroriders, also had a single screen at the front with the three number rollers and a separate destination roller. The latter also had three number rollers behind the door but these were rarely used.

With the introduction of the Lynx and Olympians three letter/number blinds were provided in the front aperture, still positioned to the right of the destination roller, thus permitting route numbers above 99 to be displayed. When route numbers had replaced letters in November 1980 the buses in use at the time were limited as to what route numbers could be displayed, since they only had two number blinds. Some of the Atlanteans were fitted with new number rolls which carried numbers 10 to 50, but these had to be smaller and thinner for the double digit numbers to fit on the rollers and consequently they spoilt the overall effect. Olympian No.(1)32 was initially an odd one out as the number blinds were to the left of the destination blind, but within six months it was returned to Northern Counties to have the rollers altered to conform with the standard. No side destination screens were included on either type of vehicle although both nearside and rear route number displays were specified on the Olympians.

The 1999 batch of Tridents, Nos. 190-6, additionally had side route number boxes, whilst the later batch, Nos. 182-9/97-9, had side destination boxes, in lieu of the number boxes, and a number box at the rear. The Tridents were also the first new buses to have blinds displaying the yellow 'Day-Glo' lettering, which was deemed to be more easily visible in the dark or in gloomy light. The first two batches of Solos, Nos. 51-8 and Nos. 59-67, had side destination screens which displayed both the route number and the destination. For over a century the blinds had been made of linen although the method of changing the destination had been made simpler by the introduction of electronically controlled blinds, which the driver could change at the touch of a button. With the introduction of the Scanias and the next batch of Solos, in August and September 2006, the first buses with LED (Light Emitting Diode) destination displays entered the fleet. These consisted of a number and destination display on the front and nearside and a route number display on the back or in the case of the Scanias a combined route and destination display on the back. Initially, the practice of displaying the front route numbers to the right of the destination was continued but later they were reconfigured and all LED fitted buses now show the route numbers on the nearside, to the left of the destination. The subsequent batches of Solos and Scanias were all fitted with LED destination displays from new.

With the exception of Lynx No. 29228, all of the buses which were transferred to Stagecoach's Frenchwood depot, which included Tridents Nos. 182/3, were fitted with LED destination equipment in order that they could work on any of the inter urban routes which worked out of the Frenchwood depot. On their return to Deepdale they retained this equipment and under Rotala ownership a slow programme of similarly equipping all the Tridents, including the acquired examples, was implemented.

The Scania Esteems were delivered new with LED destination displays although originally the route number was shown on the offside. Following the takeover by Stagecoach the 12 vehicles were numbered 28510-21 of which the first five received Stagecoach colours. No. 28519 is seen in the Royal Preston Hospital grounds in April 2009, a few weeks after Stagecoach's revised service pattern was introduced. Initially bought by Preston Bus to convert the Farringdon Park and Ribbleton Gamull Lane services to low-floor bus operation, Stagecoach transferred all but the first two to Frenchwood and initially used them on the interworked 19 and 22 services. A Solo can be seen behind on Citi route 19A which had previously been PBLs service 19, routed around the adjacent housing area. Nos. 28513/4 were retained by Stagecoach following the acquisition by Rotala. Following the service changes made by Rotala in May 2013 the original service 19 (19A under Stagecoach operation) was restricted to only a handful of early morning journeys whilst the more recent 19A (omitting Broadwood Drive & Brooklands Avenue) became the principal route.

6. Rebuilds and Modifications

The undertaking had been renowned for its ambitious tram and bus modification work and this continued for many years. It was only during the late 1990s that such work ceased to be carried out, mainly because the skilled staff required to do the work were in short supply and the few who were employed were engaged on the day to day work of keeping the buses on the road.

Tram modifications and rebuilds

The original 4-wheel cars very quickly became dated and offered no protection from the elements on the top deck. Consequently, the Corporation was authorised to go out to tender to have top covers fitted to the cars. Not surprisingly, the tender was won by the local United Electric Car Company in Strand Road where the trams had originally been built. The first batch consisted of ten cars and they were modified in 1907, at a cost of £120 each. Fitting of the covers also included the provision of new windows, in five bays, and end partition windows and doors, thus offering almost total protection from the elements, although they retained open balconies. By 1913 all but Nos. 14-6 had been so treated and it would appear that these were retained as open-top cars for continued use on the Ashton service, under Fylde Road Railway Bridge. In 1916 it was decided to fit Philipson side guards to all of the Corporation's trams, which then numbered 39, presumably to safeguard intending passengers from falling under the wheels.

In May 1924 the decision was made to carry out substantial modifications to car No. 1, whereby the open balcony ends were replaced by fully enclosed ends. Its appearance was very pleasing to the eye and the result was akin to that of a new standard type double-deck car. In all, nine of the 1904 cars were rebuilt to the same format with Nos. 5, 6, 9, 17, 19, 23-5 following in quick succession. In addition most, if not all, of the 1914 vestibule cars Nos. 34-9, were given the same treatment. A more substantial reconstruction job involved former Sheffield single-deck cars Nos. 40 and 42. Just how much of these cars was actually used for the rebuilds is unclear but the rebuilt cars were virtually new double-deck cars and were a joint venture between the Corporation and the English Electric Company, with one being turned out in 1928 and the other the following year. The new cars carried the same numbers but No. 42 was renumbered to No. 30 in 1932 to accommodate the new TD2 motorbuses. Unfortunately, No. 40 only survived for seven years, being broken up in September 1935, but No. 30(42) was sold to Lytham St Annes Corporation in August 1934 for £150 and saw several more years of service. This was the only tram which was sold to another system for further use, as all the rest were broken up.

Pre-war Titan re-bodied buses

At the Transport Committee meeting held on 17th July 1939, it was resolved to fit new bodies to five existing buses at a cost not exceeding £880 each. At the following meeting, held on 18th September, it was resolved to fit a further four buses with new bodies at a cost not exceeding £800 each. The General Manager's report had identified several of the English Electric-bodied TD2s, from the batches Nos. 41-9 and Nos. 53, 68-70, as being in need of major work. The former were only eight years old, having entered the fleet in July 1932 as the first tramway replacement vehicles, whilst the latter were a year younger having only gone into service in March 1933 or, in the case of No. 53, in October. Indeed, the latter seemed a strange choice as it was originally given an all-metal body, whereas the others had the more usual composite construction. All were re-bodied at the Strand Road English Electric Works and retained the same seating capacity of H29/24R. Towards the end of the war it was decided to fit new bodies to three of the batch of 1933 TD3s, Nos. 54-9, and three of the lowbridge 1934 TD3cs. Consequently, Nos. 9, 55/6/8 were all sent to Croft's Gallowgate factory in Glasgow for the work to be done and whilst the lowbridge vehicle gained one extra seat on the top deck, the other three were up-seated by two in the lower saloon. However, Crofts could not fulfil the order and East Lancashire Coachbuilders of Blackburn were approached about constructing new bodies for a further two lowbridge buses but, presumably because they didn't have the capacity to carry out the work, no more were actually done (see Table 12).

No.	Reg. No.	Chassis	New Body	Date
1	CK 4921	TD3	Croft L27/26R	-/51
9*	CK 4929	TD3	Croft L27/26R	3/45
41	CK 4637	TD2	E.E. H29/24R	3/40
43	CK 4639	TD2	E.E. H29/24R	8/40
44	CK 4640	TD2	E.E. H29/24R	4/40
45	CK 4641	TD2	E.E. H29/24R	9/40
46	CK 4642	TD2	E.E. H29/24R	3/40
47	CK 4643	TD2	E.E. H29/24R	6/40
49	CK 4646	TD2	E.E. H29/24R	5/40
53	CK 4702	TD2	E.E. H29/24R	7/40
55	CK 4793	TD3	Croft H29/26R	3/45
56	CK 4794	TD3	Croft H29/26R	3/45
58	CK 4796	TD3	Croft H29/26R	12/45
69	CK 4704	TD2	E.E. H29/24R	12/40

Table 12

* No. 9 was withdrawn in January 1951 and its Croft body was transferred to No. 1 which was the last of the batch to be withdrawn.

Lion Ambulance conversions

At the Committee meeting held on 20th April 1939, it was agreed to equip four single-deck buses for use as First Aid Mobile Units, at a cost of £12 each. The buses used were the 1928 batch of Leyland Lion LT1s, Nos. 71-4, which had been new in 1929. The conversions were ready in December and No. 71 was initially used by the Rural District Council before becoming the charge of the County Council. No. 72 was also used by the County Council whilst Nos. 73/4 were at the disposal of the Borough Council. At the end of the war they became surplus to requirements and were disposed of individually.

As an aside, 1932 built Lion No. 75 was loaned to the Buildings Committee and used by the Auxiliary Fire Service as a mobile canteen from December 1940 until February 1945. Again, the vehicle did not return to use with the Transport Department and was disposed of.

Pre-war Titan & Lion gearbox and engine conversions

Well over half of the pre-war Titans were fitted with torque converters from new rather than conventional gearboxes. The torque converter acted as a sort of automatic transmission but was not ideal for the rigours of urban bus driving. The buses fitted with the converters consisted of the ten 1934 lowbridge TD3s, Nos. 1-10; the 22 1935 TD4s, Nos. 11-32; the five 1938 TD5s, Nos. 33-7; the four 1940 TD5s, Nos. 4, 38-40 and the three 1936 TD4s, Nos.

62-4. There were also three Lions fitted with the converters, viz. Nos. 81-3. The first to be fitted with a crash gearbox was lowbridge No. 3, in October 1943. The conversion was deemed a success and all the rest, with six exceptions, were similarly treated over the next six years, with the programme reaching its conclusion with the three Lions in July 1949. The six buses that weren't converted were Nos. 2, 4, 5, 10, 30 and 31, all of which had been withdrawn by the end of 1950.

The nine Lions, Nos. 71-4, 75-8 and 79, were powered by 5.1 litre petrol engines; whilst the TD1s, Nos. 51/2, 60/6/7, had 6.8 litre units and the TD2s, Nos. 41-9 and 68/9, had the larger capacity 7.6 litre engines. The first of these to be converted to oil (diesel) combustion was No. 78 in December 1936, although it has not been possible to determine what size of engine it received. The remainder of the Lions and most of the TD2s were converted the following year, although the last four to be done were Nos. 41/2/4/6 in October 1939. Again, the size of engine fitted to the TDs is not confirmed although it would almost certainly have been either the 8.1 litre or the 8.6 litre unit. Nos. 50 and 70, the last of 1932 and 1933 TD2s respectively, were both received new with an 8.1 litre diesel engine but No. 50 also gained a new unit in June 1943. None of the TD1s were re-engined and No. 51 was the last petrol-engined bus in service when it was withdrawn in May 1947, having survived some seven years longer than the other TD1s.

Mobile Library Bus

At the Transport Committee meeting held on 16th February 1948 the manager reported that a request had been made from the Library & Arts Committee for the provision of a single-deck bus which was suitable to be converted into a travelling library and that he had estimated that the cost of the conversion would be £320. One of the 1932 Leyland Lions, No. 76, had been retired from service in January and it was selected as a suitable candidate. The conversion took several months to complete, but CK 4649 took up its new duties on 20th September. As part of the conversion the bus was fitted with a translucent middle section to the roof to provide natural light since its windows were removed and panelled over to accommodate the longitudinal book shelving. The Lion performed this role until November 1966, when it was replaced by a purpose-built Bedford vehicle. It was a common

Original 1904 4-wheel car No. 24 is seen in its final rebuilt form on Fishergate Bridge outside the Central Railway Station. It appears to be showing route letter 'O' denoting 'Other' service and may well be a special car for PNE's football ground, some of which started here. One of the 1932 TD2s is seen passing behind the tram returning from Penwortham (Broadgate) not long after the service was converted to motorbus operation.

In 1945 it was resolved to fit new bodies to six of the 1933 and 1934 TD3s. The original intention was to treat three of the lowbridge types but in the event only No. 9 was done at Crofts in Glasgow. However, No. 9 was withdrawn in 1951 so the relatively new body was then mounted on the chassis of No. 1. The bus is seen outside Saul Street baths on Baths Special duty in the early 1950s, a duty which the undertaking has performed from 1938 to the present day.

sight parked in Jacson Street, alongside the Harris Library, where it was loaded with new selections of books. The bus is believed to be still in existence and has changed hands more than once as a long-term preservation project.

Pre-war Titan conversions to Mobile Grandstands

Preston Guild is a festival held once every 20 years and culminates in a week long celebration at the beginning of September, during which several large processions are staged around the city (town) centre. In 1952 the Corporation had the idea of using some redundant buses as grandstands, which could be readily positioned on the procession route. Several TDs were in store at the depot, having been withdrawn at various times during the previous two years. The vehicles chosen for the conversions were TD3 No. 54; TD4s, Nos. 15 and 27; TD5s, Nos. 33 and 36 and TD2 No. 43. The latter had been new in June 1932 and was one of the buses which had been re-bodied in 1940. All of the batch were withdrawn between December 1950 and February 1951, except for No. 50 which had been retired some years earlier. Despite being the first to be taken out of service, No. 43 had survived in use with the undertaking as a driver training vehicle. The six buses were substantially modified for their new role. All the windows were removed on the nearside and the window apertures were enlarged at the top. A narrow canopy was constructed above the upper deck window apertures to afford some protection from adverse weather. Inside, three longitudinal seats were created on each deck, with each row slightly higher than the one in front. The leather seat cushions from the original seats were reused and laid lengthwise. The stands were given individual numbers from 1 to 6. From photographs, stands Nos. 1, 3, 5 and 6 have been clearly identified as being former buses Nos. 54, 33, 15 and 43 respectively but it has so far not been possible to confirm which stand numbers the remaining two buses carried.

It was decided to give the mobile stands a test run before the main Guild event and four of them were taken down to the cricket ground at West Cliff and used as spectator stands during a County Cricket match between Lancashire and Glamorgan, over the three day period 18th to 20th June. The stands were deemed a success and all six were used for the main event, from the 1st to 6th September, and were reportedly positioned around the open area at Kendal Street and Corporation Street. Since all the vehicles had had their engines removed they were towed to the two events. At the end of the Guild the Corporation had no further use for them and all were sold for scrap, with Nos. 15, 27, 33 and 36 going to a local merchant and Nos. 43 and 54 going to a scrap merchant in Salford.

PD2/10 Rebuilding Programme

The Corporation had always had a requirement for lowbridge buses to work the main Ashton service under Fylde Road Railway Bridge. However, in the summer of 1957, the road was lowered under the bridge thus permitting highbridge buses to pass underneath. The lowbridge PD2s were relatively new buses and the seating arrangement on the top deck consisted of long cross seats, accessed from a sunken gangway on the offside. This arrangement was awkward for both passengers and the conductors alike. Consequently, at the Transport Committee meeting held on 13th March 1959, it was resolved to convert two of the lowbridge buses to the format of a conventional PD3. On reflection this was a very ambitious undertaking as the buses required not only increasing in width and length but also in height. The estimated cost of carrying out two conversions was £2,000 per vehicle. This was considered very reasonable given that the cost of the new PD3s (Nos. 62-8) had been in the region of £6,000 per vehicle.

Number 9 was chosen as the first bus to be modified and was taken into the bodyshop almost immediately. Over the next eight months it underwent a major transformation to increase the vehicle dimensions from 7ft 6ins to 8ft 0ins wide, 26ft 10ins to 30ft long and 13ft 6ins to 14ft 6ins (in practice the former lowbridge buses were increased to 14ft 2ins) in height. Some of the tasks involved to achieve this included the provision of new main and cross members to the chassis; a new wider front axle; a longer drive shaft and the fitting of stronger springs to carry the extra weight. The new bodywork was then built up on the enlarged chassis, with the lower deck being assembled first. The new roof and upper deck were constructed separately from the vehicle and fitted as a complete unit. No. 9 originally had twenty-seven seats on the upper deck and twenty-eight on the lower deck; in its rebuilt form this was greatly increased to forty-one

The TD2s were originally powered by 7.6 litre petrol engines but these were replaced by oil (diesel) engines in the late 1930s. No. 44 was one of the last to be changed in October 1939 whilst Nos. 45 and 48 were changed over in February and April 1937, respectively.

1932 Leyland Lion No. 76, in its new guise as a Travelling Library, is seen at one of its usual haunts in Winmarleigh Road close to the Ashton Pedders Lane terminus. The library had ten regular sites which it visited during the course of each week. CK 4649 was replaced by a purpose-built Bedford SB vehicle in 1966 although the bus is thought to be still in existence.

An inside view of the vehicle showing the purpose-built book shelving and translucent roof. The bus could be seen on a daily basis parked in Jacson Street alongside the Harris library where the stock of books would be changed and the librarians would prepare the vehicle for another day's work.

The six TDs used as mobile grandstands for the 1952 Preston Guild are seen lined up on the 'Moor'. From the front they are stands Nos. 5(15), 4(36), 2(27), 6(43), 1(54) and 3(33). The fleet numbers are shown in brackets but it has so far not been possible to positively identify Stands 2 & 4 although the vehicles used are known. Four of the stands were first trialled at a cricket match at West Cliff in June before the main event at the end of August. They were positioned on the processional route around Kendal Street and Corporation Street and entry was by ticket only which had the number of the stand printed on it. The seats inside were formed longitudinally and the original seat cushions were used lengthwise. The buses were all sold for scrap after the Guild.

Three views which were taken during the rebuilding of the first PD2, No. 9.

Work is progressing on the construction of the lower deck, including the ceiling and front entrance. Already a newly reconditioned 0.600 engine has been fitted.

The upper deck and roof was constructed as a single separate section, before being lowered on to the lower deck section. Once attached, a new floor for the upper deck was constructed and wiring for the lights and bell pushes fitted before the internal panel work was completed.

In the bottom picture the large proportions of the finished vehicle contrast markedly with those of No. 10, still in its original PD2 form. The extended wheelbase of the original chassis is clearly evident. Nos. 9 and 10 are posed on the 'Moor' in December 1959.

and thirty-two respectively. Whereas the original vehicle had an open back platform, the new vehicle had a pneumatically operated front sliding door. The whole project was deemed a resounding success and the final cost had come out at a respectable 12% over estimate. The second authorised rebuild was to No. 5 and work was commenced straight after No. 9 had been completed and it again took about eight months to complete. The seating layout on the top deck was somewhat simplified and was reduced by three. Nos. 2 and 10 followed to the same specifications and all four were in service by February 1962.

The Transport Committee had been so impressed with the conversions that it was decided to rebuild some normal height PD2s to the same PD3 specification. Whilst Nos. 50 and 51 followed fairly rapidly the last two were completed some time after they were first authorised. It is somewhat surprising that the last one, No. 59, actually went ahead as by the time it was taken out of service, around December 1966, the Committee had already decided on a policy of buying new single-deck buses for 'PAYB' operation. The highbridge models were slightly easier to convert as they didn't require any alteration to their height. No. 59 entered service in September 1967, by which time the livery had been changed from maroon and cream to blue and ivory and so consequently it was the only PD3 which never wore maroon. All eight were withdrawn from service between June 1977 (No. 9) and March 1979 (No. 2); the latter and No. 61 are both preserved (see Table 13).

Breakdown Vehicles

Prior to 1960 a purpose-built recovery vehicle had latterly been used to rescue broken down vehicles and carry out other sundry duties. At the Committee meeting held on 15th August 1960 it was resolved to convert an obsolete lowbridge bus for use as a breakdown vehicle. The bus concerned was accident victim, PD1 No. 6. The bus was cut down to little more than the cab and the first two lower deck bays; the chassis was shortened and the lifting gear from the previous breakdown vehicle was mounted behind what was left of the lower saloon. The new recovery vehicle was ready for use in April 1962 and continued to operate under the same trade plates, 061 CK. In September 1977 it was retired from front line duty and replaced by former PD3/4, No. 16, which was similarly cut down for its new role in life. Yet again the lifting gear was transferred from the outgoing vehicle as were the trade plates. Carrying the number R1 it took over recovery duties in March 1978. It was renumbered to 100 in November 1983 and re-registered to Q644 GFV in January 1988. In 1993 a brand new Seddon Atkinson purpose-built Strato 400 recovery vehicle was acquired and No. 100 was eventually stood down that September. During 2011 the Atkinson underwent a comprehensive overhaul and in December it was fully repainted at Walsall into an all-over green colour scheme with front and back red & yellow chevrons. At times ordinary buses have been used to perform towing duties when the recovery vehicle has not been available. PS1 No. 74, National No. 5 and Atlantean No. 181 are three buses which are known to have been used in such circumstances.

PD1 & PS1 Polling Station conversions

Seven PD1s had been withdrawn during 1963; No. 84 was retired in May and Nos. 72/3, 85/6 and 95/6 were rendered surplus to requirements in November when the seven new PD3A/1s Nos. 84-90 entered service. At the Committee meeting held on 20th January 1964 it was resolved to carry out a conversion of one bus for use as a mobile Polling Station, at an estimated cost of £80. Actual details of the conversions are not to hand but it can be assumed that the lower deck seating was removed to create space for a desk for the clerks employed to check the voters' register and somewhere in

	Table 13					
C'ttee Resolution	Estimated Cost(£)	Vehicle No.	Reg No.	New Reg No.	To service	Withdrawn
13th March 1959	2,000*	9	FRN 731	NCK 741	02/11/59	16/06/77
13th March 1959	2,000	5	ECK 510	NCK 757	--/07/60	24/12/78
15th August 1960	2,250	2	ECK 509	PRN 761	--/07/61	31/03/79
15th August 1960	2,250	10	FRN 732	PRN 762	--/02/62	31/07/77
10th March 1962	2,322	50	FRN 734	SRN 375	--/12/62	31/01/78
10th March 1962	2,322	51	FRN 735	SRN 376	--/08/63	30/09/77
19th August 1963	2,350	61	FRN 740	BCK 367C	02/04/65	30/03/78
19th August 1963	2,350	59	FRN 739	FCK 453F	--/09/67	11/10/78
*Actual cost of the conversion was reported to be £2,283						

seclusion for the voter to mark their ballot paper. The stairs to the top deck were blanked off and the lower deck windows were partially masked out. Finally, the engine and gearbox were both removed and consequently the vehicles had to be towed to their sites. The conversion was considered a success and four more buses were similarly treated, with Nos. 72/3, 85/6 and 98 making up the total complement. The five buses were transferred to the Policy & Resources Committee in August but may well not have been used until the following May, the usual time of the year for local elections. They are recorded as being out of use by 1969 but their disposals are not known. That, however, was not the end of the Polling Station conversions since

Leyland Tiger No. 74 was modified for a similar role and was first used for the General Election in June 1970. It was regularly used at a site in Salmon Street, off London Road, and is believed to have last been used for the 1979 May local elections. No. 74 later passed into preservation and returned to the depot in July 1983 for repainting into the original maroon and cream livery.

Training Buses

Over the years a number of buses have been used as Driver Training Vehicles. Sometimes they would perform this role whilst still remaining licensed as a psv, whilst others have undergone work to convert them into permanent Tuition Vehicles (see Table 14).

Table 14

No.	Reg.	Type	Dates	Notes
70	CK 4705	TD2	9/48 to 12/50	
43	CK 4639	TD2	1/51 to -/52	Subsequently converted to a Guild Grandstand.
8	BCK 25	PD1	c3/60 to 5/60	Renumbered from 60 in 3/58.
72	BCK 622	PD1	10/61	
97	BCK 631	PD1	1960s	
35	KRN 426	PD2/10	4/71 to 9/71	
37	KRN 428	PD2/10	1960s	
43	ECK 503	PD2/10	1/72 to 11/74	Permanent conversion with glazing to upper deck side windows removed and apertures panelled over.
54	FRN 737	PD2/10	1/76 to 3/80	Permanent Driver Trainer and numbered TU1.
57	FRN 738	PD2/10	1/76 to 3/80	Permanent Driver Trainer.
117	DRN 300	PD2/1	7/70 to 10/70	
125	DRN 308	PD2/1	4/73 to 10/75	Permanent Driver Trainer.
127	DRN 310	PD2/1	1950s/1960s	Used as a psv and training bus at the same time.
17	PRN 909	PD3/5	6/80 to 11/94	Permanent conversion with top deck isolated and repainted into a mainly ivory livery. Originally numbered T1; renumbered to 99 in 10/83 and re-registered to PFF 997 in 11/94 prior to disposal.
19	PRN 911	PD3/5	3/80 to 1/84	Modified as T1 and numbered T2.
68/9	D768/9 YCW	Dodge	from 5/87	Mini-bus driver familiarisation.
224	H24 YBV	Lynx	7/96	Used for one day only on 11th July.
173	DRN 173Y	AN68	7/96 to 6/97 & from 1/01	
175	DRN 175Y	AN68	10/96 to c4/02	
176	DRN 176Y	AN68	6/97 to 8/98	
181	DRN 1Y	AN68	8/97	Renumbered from 1 in 11/94.
182	DRN 2Y	AN68	5/97 to 6/97	Renumbered from 2 in 11/94 and to 180 in 8/00.
51/3/4/6	PE51 YHF/H/J/L	Solo	12/01	Driver familiarisation.
133	A33 MRN	ON	2/02 to 6/05	Renumbered from 33 in 3/95; originally 3.
100	F32 AHG	ON	6/05 & from 4/07	Renumbered from 132 in 2/05; originally 32.
201	PL06 RYO	Scania	8/06	Driver familiarisation.
136	G36 OCK	ON	from 6/05	Renumbered from 36 in 4/95.
31082	K128 UFV	Delta	from 2/08	Acquired from Blackpool Transport and converted for use as a permanent Driver Training Vehicle; numbered 26082 by Stagecoach in 1/09 and renumbered by Rotala to 31082 in 9/11.
30124	YJ61 JJF	Versa	12/11	Driver familiarisation
31215	G215 KRN	Lynx	5/12	Used for two days on 15th & 16th May.
40606/7/8	PR62 TON, PO62 LNU/F	Volvo	12/12	Driver familiarisation

Hired buses used :- Dodge D912 NBA 3-4/87; Fr Rov Dormobile D861/2 LWR 3-5/87; Optare Delta K130 UFV in 12/11.

The 1947 Chevrolet, carrying Trade plates 061 CK, is engaged in removing the bus shelters from Fishergate Bridge in February 1958, prior to British Rail carrying out a full re-decking of the bridge which required the road to be closed for nearly eight months. The Chevrolet was normally used for vehicle recoveries but was obviously evidently used for other duties. The Art Deco building in the background was then a car showroom but has had many different uses over the years including in more recent times as a Japanese Sushi Bar.

The lifting gear from the Chevrolet was transferred to the new breakdown vehicle, former PD1 No. 6 (originally 106), in 1962 and it continued to operate using the same trade plates until 1977. It is seen on the 'Moor' demonstrating its towing and lifting capabilities with the aid of Leyland PD2/1 No. 115. A number of PD1s can be seen parked behind, facing the garage wall.

A rare picture of one of the Polling Stations actually in use at the junction of Ashworth Grove and the Boulevard, in Frenchwood. Note the 'On Tow' chalked on the back of the vehicle.

All five conversions are visible in this view taken on the 'Moor' at the back of No. 4 garage. Unfortunately, the practice of painting out the fleet numbers and removing the registration plates makes individual identification impossible other than No. 86 which is on the end of the row beyond the PD2.

1949-built Leyland Tiger No. 74 is seen at its regular Salmon Street location in use as a Mobile Polling Station. Unlike the PD1 conversions the engine was not removed and the bus was driven to site. It was used as such throughout the 1970s and went on to become the subject of a preservation project.

New in March 1954 and converted for use as a Training Vehicle in January 1976, No. 54 was withdrawn from such duties on 24th March 1980. Seen a month later it has been borrowed by the Bus Stop repair gang. Along with sister vehicle No. 57, which was also used as a Trainer over the same period, the two buses were sold to C F Booth at Rotherham where they were scrapped a couple of months later.

Following the use of several Atlanteans and Olympians for short durations, a permanent Training Vehicle in the form of a DAF Optare Excel was purchased from Blackpool Transport in February 2008. Dating from January 1993 K128 UFV is seen in Fishergate three months after entering service. Initially it was not allocated a fleet number until acquired by Stagecoach when it became 26082. Under the Rotala scheme it was renumbered to 31082.

7. Depot Developments

Depot Development Dates

1904	A new tram car shed, offices and a generating station were opened in Holmrook Road, off Deepdale Road.
1915	New offices, incorporating an extension to the car shed, were built fronting Deepdale Road.
1925	A small garage was built at the rear of the car shed to garage some of the single deck buses.
1926	The generating station was closed with power henceforth being taken from the then new Ribble Power Station.
1932	An extension was built to the side of the car shed to house the expanding bus fleet; this included an inspection area (No. 3).
1933	The two tram roads nearest to the bus garage were concreted in to provide additional bus parking space.
1936	The car shed was reconfigured with steel girders replacing the stanchions and the floor concreted in for bus parking.
1944	A heated pipe system was installed in the garage yard to prevent the radiators from freezing up.
1950s	A bus sprinkler washing system was installed in No. 1 garage.
1954	A high pressure chassis cleaner was installed in the garage yard.
c`1958	The heating pipe system in the yard was removed.
1964	A new covered extension was opened at the back of Nos.1 and 2 garages and was known as No. 4.
1965	Part of No. 1 (the original car shed) was fitted out as a docking shop with new pits etc.
Unknown	A new mechanical bus wash was installed in the far corner of No. 4 garage.
1977	The remainder of No. 1 garage was equipped as a bodyshop; a new bus wash was installed in No. 4 garage.
1983	The boiler house chimney was demolished.
1986	A new bus wash was installed in No. 4 garage nearer to the entrance.
1989	A gated compound was constructed in the yard to house mini-buses.
2008	The compound was removed.

This interesting picture shows an assortment of buses parked up against the heated pipe system in the garage yard. It is highly likely that this view dates from 1957 as several of the buses depicted are now painted in the 1956 livery. On view are 1940 Leyland-bodied TD5c No. 4, 1947 lowbridge Leyland-bodied PD1A No. 107 and 1950 all Leyland PD2/1 No. 115. On the other side of the system is a highbridge PD1 and out of sight (identified from another photograph) next to the PD1 is the last lowbridge TD3c No. 1, which was withdrawn in September 1957. It is believed that the heating system was removed in 1958 but it is not known whether it was still in use as such right through to its demise.

The first mechanical bus wash of any description consisted simply of an overhead sprinkler system which was situated near the entrance to No. 1 garage. Sometime in the 1960s this was superseded by a fully automatic wash which was situated in the far corner of the then new No. 4 garage. This was replaced in 1977 by an updated model which lasted until 1986. Both of these washes had employed the principle whereby the bus remained static and the brushes moved

along and over the vehicle. The present wash, seen right, was positioned more centrally so that the buses could be driven through. Wrightbus-bodied Volvo hybrid No. 40622 passes through the wash on 7th May 2013, some two months before it actually entered service.

A view inside the front of No.1 garage circa 1967. 1952 Leyland-bodied PD2/10 No. 47 was painted blue and ivory in March of that year, whilst 1951 PD2/1 No. 122 behind was painted in May of the following year and was one of only five of the batch which received this livery. This part of No. 1 was converted into the bodyshop in 1977.

Number 3 garage was a small inspection building built on the side of No.2 garage , both of which were opened in 1932. This view, which is believed to date from 1933, shows three of the Corporation's Leyland Lions. The two front entrance vehicles are Leyland-bodied LT1s which were new in September 1929 with No.73 on the left. The vehicle in the middle is English Electric-bodied LT5 No.78 which was then only a year old. Although somewhat altered this building is still in use as a vehicle inspection area and there is what appears to be the original No.3 plaque attached to the opposite face of the large central pillar.

In this 5th September 2013 view an assortment of vehicles can be seen parked up in No.4 garage, between duties. This vast cathedral like garage was opened in the spring of 1964 and was built on land at the back of No.1 and No.2 garages. From left to right are former Stagecoach London Alexander-bodied Dennis Trident No.40601, Optare Versa hybrid No.30122, ELC-bodied Dennis Trident No.40599 and Leyland-bodied Olympians Nos. 42559/60, with the former sporting the Guild 2012 livery.

In 1977 a new bodyshop was established at the front of No.1 garage. The rear section of this garage had previously been converted to a docking shop in 1965. Optare Metrorider No.18 is seen in the bodyshop in May 2008, having been stripped down following an accident which had occurred outside the garage a few days earlier. The bus was deemed to be uneconomical to repair and the remains were sold to scrap merchant Trevor Wigley. This part of the depot was constructed in 1915 as an extension to the original tram shed.

The building which became the paintshop was originally the boiler house and was situated next to the generator room where the electricity to power the tram system was generated. Whilst the Corporation ceased to generate their own power after 1926 it is not known exactly when it was converted to a paintshop. The entrance was originally from an open yard until garage No.4 was built on the site of the open area in 1964. This view shows Leyland Olympian No.107 in April 1999 when it was used to trial several different colour schemes before a new arrangement of blue and cream was chosen for a new fleet livery. Following the repainting of the same vehicle into PB Rotala colours in September 2011, in-house painting of the buses ceased and all subsequent repaints have been done by specialist outside concerns.

A view inside the docking shop which was previously No.1 garage and originally the tramcar shed which dates from 1904. Seddon Pennine-bodied Panther No. 223 and Marshall Camair-bodied example No. 238 are seen undergoing attention in February 1981, along with ELC-bodied Atlantean No.130.

In an area of the 'Moor' once referred to as the Cemetery (for obvious reasons) a collection of withdrawn PD3/As can be seen covered in a thick blanket of snow on 21st January 1979. The buses on view are Nos. 64, 88, 84, 87 and 62, all of which had been withdrawn between May and November 1978. Nos. 62, 84/7 passed to Geoff Lister at Bolton, No. 88 was acquired by D Rollinson at Carlton and No. 64 gained a reprieve being one of the two buses which passed to Brown & Root as semi-preserved vehicles.

Buses Operated 1922-2013

Nos.	Registration	Chassis	Body	Seating	Dates	Notes
51-3	CK 3446/5/7	Leyland G7	English Electric	B30D	1/22	
54	CK 3512	Leyland G7	English Electric	B30D	6/23	
55-9	CK 3563/4/0-2	Leyland SG7	English Electric	B36D	6/24	1
60/1	CK 3629/30	Leyland A13	English Electric	B22D	3/25	
62	CK 3631	Leyland SG9	English Electric	B26D	3/25	
63/4	CK 3746/5	Leyland LSP1	Leyland	H30/22RO	8/26	2
65	CK 3907	Leyland LSP2	Leyland	H45RO	12/27	2
1-10	CK 4921-30	Leyland TD3c	English Electric	L26/26R	8/34	3, 4
11-4	RN 7701-4	Leyland TD4c	Leyland	H30/24R	11/35	5, 6
15-32	RN 7705-22	Leyland TD4c	English Electric	H28/26R	11/35-12/35	
33-7	RN 8348-52	Leyland TD5c	English Electric	H30/24R	12/37	6
38-40	RN 8885/6/4	Leyland TD5c	Leyland	H29/26R	4/39	6
41-50	CK 4637-44/6/7	Leyland TD2	English Electric	H29/24R	7/32	7, 6
51/2	CK 4601/2	Leyland TD1	English Electric	H29/24R	10/31	
53	CK 4702	Leyland TD2	English Electric	H27/24R	10/33	5, 6
54-9	CK 4792-7	Leyland TD3	English Electric	H29/24R	11/33	6
60	OF 3959	Leyland TD1	Leyland	L24/24R	3/35	8
61	TJ 3278	Leyland TD3c	Leyland	H30/26R	3/35	5, 8
62-4	RN 8018-20	Leyland TD4c	English Electric	H30/24R	9/36	6
65	ACK 224	Leyland TD7	Leyland	H30/26R	3/40	
66	CK 4050	Leyland TD1	Leyland	L24/24RO	9/28	
67	CK 4172	Leyland TD1	Leyland	L24/24RO	8/29	
68-70	CK 4703-5	Leyland TD2	English Electric	H28/24R	3/33	9
71-4	CK 4173-6	Leyland LT1	Leyland	B35F	9/29	
75-8	CK 4648-51	Leyland LT5	English Electric	B32R	7/32	10
79	CK 4706	Leyland LT5	English Electric	B32R	3/33	10
80	CK 4707	Leyland TS4	English Electric	B32R	3/33	10
81/2	RN 7723/4	Leyland LT7c	Leyland	B38R	11/35	5
83	RN 8353	Leyland LT7c	English Electric	B38R	12/37	
4	RN 8887	Leyland TD5c	Leyland	L27/26R	1/40	11
52	ARN 394	Leyland PD1	Alexander%	H30/26R	9/46	
60/6/7	BCK 25-7	Leyland PD1	Leyland	L27/26R	12/46	12
71-3	BCK 621-3	Leyland PD1A	Leyland	H30/26R	5/47	
74/5	CRN 79, 80	Leyland PS1	East Lancs	B36R	6/49	13
84-9	ARN 388-93	Leyland PD1	Alexander%	H30/26R	7/46-9/46	
90-4	BCK 624-8	Leyland PD1A	Leyland	H30/26R	5/47	14
95-100	BCK 629-34	Leyland PD1A	Samlesbury%	H30/26R	9/47-10/47	
101/2	BCK 635/6	Leyland PD1A	Leyland	H30/26R	10/47	
103-7	BCK 936-40	Leyland PD1A	Leyland	L27/26R	8/47	12, 15
2, 5	ECK 509/10	Leyland PD2/10	Leyland	L27/28R	3/52	
9, 10	FRN 731/2	Leyland PD2/10	Leyland	L27/28R	3/54	
20-2	KCK 328-30	Leyland PD2/10	Crossley	H32/26R	3/57	16
24-8	JCK 583-7	Leyland PD2/10	Crossley	H30/28R	6/56-7/56	16
23/9-37	KRN 419-28	Leyland PD2/10	Crossley	H32/26R	8/57-12/57	16
41-8	ECK 501-8	Leyland PD2/10	Leyland	H30/28R	2/52-3/52	16
49-51/3 /4/7/9, 61	FRN 733-40	Leyland PD2/10	Leyland	H30/28R	3/54	16
79-83	KRN 485-9	Leyland PD2/10	MCW	H32/26R	10/55	16
108-27	DRN 291-310	Leyland PD2/1	Leyland	H30/26R	12/50-2/51	17
2≠	PRN 761	Leyland PD3/6	Leyland/PCTD	H38/32F	7/61	
5≠	NCK 757	Leyland PD3/6	Leyland/PCTD	H38/32F	7/60	
9≠	NCK 741	Leyland PD3/6	Leyland/PCTD	H41/32F	11/59	
10≠	PRN 762	Leyland PD3/6	Leyland/PCTD	H38/32F	2/62	
13-9	PRN 905-11	Leyland PD3/4	MCW	H39/31F	9/61	
50/1≠	SRN 375/6	Leyland PD3/6	Leyland/PCTD	H38/32F	12/62, 8/63	
59≠	FCK 453F	Leyland PD3/6	Leyland/PCTD	H38/32F	9/67	
61≠	BCK 367C	Leyland PD3/6	Leyland/PCTD	H38/32F	4/65	
62-8	MCK 293-9	Leyland PD3/5	MCW	H40/32F	12/58	18
69-73	ARN 654-8C	Leyland PD3A/1	MCW	H39/31F	2/65-3/65	
84-90	TRN 386-92	Leyland PD3A/1	MCW	H39/31F	11/63	
201-5	HCK 201-5G	Leyland PSUR1A/1	MCW	B47D	6/68-9/68	
206-15	HCK 206-15G	Leyland PSUR1A/1	Marshall	B47D	11/68	
216-22	KRN 216-22H	Leyland PSUR1A/1R	Marshall	B49D	2/70-3/70	
223-9	MCK 223-9J	Leyland PSUR1B/1R	Seddon Pennine	B48D	4/71-5/71	
230-4	AUE 309-13J	Leyland PSUR1A/1R	Marshall Camair	B41D	11/71	19
230-6	RTF 430-6L	Leyland PSUR1B/1R	Seddon Pennine	B48D	7/72	20
242	PHG 242P	Bristol LHS	Duple	DP31F	5/76	21
243/4	PHG 243/4P	Bristol LHS	Duple	B31F	5/76	21
101-10	GBV 101-10N	Leyland AN68/2R	Alexander AL	H49/33D	12/74-2/75	
111-20	UFV 111-20R	Leyland AN68/2R	East Lancs	H50/32D	9/76-11/76	22
121-30	CRN 121-30S	Leyland AN68A/2R	East Lancs	H50/32D	10/77-1/78	
131-40	NCK 131-40T	Leyland AN68A/2R	East Lancs	H50/32D	12/78-6/79	23
141-50	UHG 141-50V	Leyland AN68A/2R	Alexander AL	H49/33D	2/80-3/80	24
151-7	GFV 151-7W	Leyland AN68B/2R	East Lancs	H50/32D	4/81	25

Nos.	Registration	Chassis	Body	Seating	Dates	Notes
158-65	OBV 158-65X	Leyland AN68B/2R	East Lancs	H50/32D	10/81-12/81	25
166-72	URN 166-72Y	Leyland AN68D/2R	East Lancs	H50/32D	10/82-12/82	25
173-7	DRN 173-7Y	Leyland AN68D/2R	East Lancs	H50/32D	5/83-6/83	25
1, 2	DRN 1,2Y	Leyland AN68D/2R	East Lancs	CH45/29F	6/83	26
3	A33 MRN	Leyland ONTL11/2R	ECW	CH47/27F	2/84	27
5-8	YFY 1, 2, 7, 8M	Leyland Nat 1151/2R/0402	Leyland	B49F	8/86	28
6	D456 BEO	Dodge S56	East Lancs	B22F	1/91	29
7	D32 SAO	Dodge S56	Reeve Burgess	B23F	1/91	29
8, 9	D458/9 BEO	Dodge S56	East Lancs	DP22F	1/91	29
40	D40 AFV	Leyland TRBTL11/2RP	Duple	C51F	5/87	30
41-3	D41-3 AFV	Dodge S56	N Counties	B22F	6/87	
44	E44 FFV	Dodge S56	N Counties	B20F	8/87	31
45/6	E45/6 GRN	Dodge S56	N Counties	B22F	10/87	
47-9	E47 KBV, E48/9 MCK	Renault S56	N Counties	B25F	2/88-3/88	
50-66	D750-66 YCW	Dodge S56	N Counties	B22F	4/87	32
67	D767 YCW	Dodge S56	N Counties	DP20F	5/87	31
68/9	D768/9 YCW	Dodge S46	N Counties	B22F	4/87	
70/1	D870/1 ABV	Dodge S56	N Counties	DP20F	5/87	31
72-4	D72-4 AFV	Dodge S56	N Counties	B22F	6/87	
75-7	E75-7 LFR	Renault S56	N Counties	B25F	2/88	
78-87	E78-87 MHG	Renault S56	N Counties	B25F	4/88-5/88	
88-90	F88-90 UHG	Renault S56	N Counties	B25F	11/88	
91/2	F91/2 AHG	Renault S56	N Counties	B25F	4/89	33
10/1	F210/1 YHG	Leyland LX2R11C15Z4R	Leyland	B47F	3/89	34
12/3	F212/3 YHG	Leyland LX2R11C15Z4R	Leyland	DP45F	3/89	34
14-8	G214-8 KRN	Leyland LX2R11C15Z4R	Leyland	DP45F	11/89	35
219/20	J921/2 MKC	Leyland LX2R11C15Z4R	Leyland Mk2	B51F	7/03	36
221/2	J925/8 MKC	Leyland LX2R11C15Z4R	Leyland Mk2	B51F	4/03	36
23/4/6-9	H23/4/6-9 YBV	Leyland LX2R11C15Z4R	Leyland	DP45F	11/90-12/90	37
32	F32 AHG	Leyland ONCL10/2RZ	N Counties	H51/34F	3/89	38
34/5	G34/5 OCK	Leyland ONCL10/1RZ	Leyland	CH43/29F	3/90	39
36/7	G36/7 OCK	Leyland ONCL10/1RZ	Leyland	H47/31F	3/90-4/90	39
101-4	H101-4 BFR	Leyland ON2R50C13Z4	N Counties	H47/30F	3/91	
106	J976 PRW	Leyland ON2R50C13Z4	Leyland	H47/31F	3/92	40
107/14	J107/14 KCW	Leyland ON2R50C13Z4	Leyland	CH43/29F	10/91, 3/92	41
108-10/2/3	J108-10/2/3 KCW	Leyland ON2R50C13Z4	Leyland	H47/31F	2/92	42
1-10	M401-10 TCK	Optare MR37	Optare	B25F	11/94-3/95	43
11-6	P411-6 TFR	Optare MR37	Optare	B25F	10/96-11/96	
17-9	R417-9 RCW	Optare MR17	Optare	B29F	6/98	44
20-31	N420-31 GBV	Optare MR17	Optare	B29F	8/95-2/96	
32-7	R432-7 NFR	Optare MR17	Optare	B29F	10/97-4/98	
38-40	R438-40 RCW	Optare MR17	Optare	B29F	7/98	43
41/2	J697/9 CGK	Optare MR03	Optare	B26F	11/00	45
182-9/97-9	X182-9/97-9 RRN	Dennis Trident 2	ELC Lolyne	H45/30F	10/00-12/00	46
190-6	V190-6 EBV	Dennis Trident 2	ELC Lolyne	H45/30F	11/99-12/99	47
323	T894 HBF	Volvo B10M-62	Van Hool	C53F	2/03	48
123-32	E323-32 MSG	Leyland ONCL10/2RZ	Alexander RH	H51/30D	3/05-4/05	49
51-8	PE51 YHF-H/J-N	Optare M850	Optare	B29F	12/01	50
59-67	PN52 ZVH/J-M/O/P/R/S	Optare M850	Optare	B29F	11/02	51
68-71	PO56 RNY/Z, ROH/U	Optare M850	Optare	B28F	9/06	
72-6	PO56 RPU/V/X-Z	Optare M850	Optare	B28F	9/06	
77/8	PN07 NTK/L	Optare M880	Optare	B28F	6/07	
79, 80	PN57 NFF/G	Optare M880	Optare	B28F	11/07	
81-3	PE55 WMD/F/G	Optare M920	Optare	B32F	12/05	
84-8	PO56 RRU/V/X-Z	Optare M920	Optare	B32F	9/06	
89-91	PO56 RSU/V/X	Optare M920	Optare	B32F	9/06	
92-7	PN07 NTJ/M/O/T/U/V	Optare M950	Optare	B32F	6/07-7/07	
151/2	PO56 RSY/Z	Scania Omnidekka	ELC	H47/33F	12/06-1/07	
200	PRN 909	Scania N230UB	ELC Esteem	B40F	10/07	
201/2	PL06 RYO/P	Scania N94UB	ELC Esteem	B41F	8/06	
203-7	PO56 JDF/J/K/U/X	Scania N94UB	ELC Esteem	B41F	8/06	52
208-11	PN57 NFA/C-E	Scania N230UB	ELC Esteem	B40F	9/07-12/07	
1-8	PN08 SVK/L/O/P/R-U	Optare M950 SR	Optare	B32F	4/08-5/08	51
28522	BF60 OEV	Mercedes 0530LE	Mercedes Citaro	B42F	2/11	
18540-4	V540-4 ESC	Dennis Trident	Plaxton President	H45/29F	4/11	53
20907/9	DRZ 4018, BRZ 9662	Wrightbus Streetlite	Wrightbus	B37F	7/12	54
20908	CRZ 7495	Wrightbus Streetlite	Wrightbus	B33F	8/12	

Nos.	Registration	Chassis	Body	Seating	Dates	Notes
30122-7	YJ61 JJU/E/F/K/L/O	Optare Versa Hybrid	Optare	B36F	12/11-1/12	
30128	YJ12 GUA	Optare Versa Hybrid	Optare	B36F	3/12	55
40600/1	X388/5 NNO	Dennis Trident	Alexander ALX400	H45/30F	12/11	56
40606	PR62 TON	Volvo B5LH Hybrid	Wrightbus Gemini 2	H45/26F	11/12	
40607-9	PO62 LNU/F/N	Volvo B5LH Hybrid	Wrightbus Gemini 2	H45/26F	11/12-12/12	
40619-21	PE13 JYY/Z/ZA	Volvo B5LH Hybrid	Wrightbus Gemini 2	H45/26F	3/13-4/13	
40622	PF13 XAC	Volvo B5LH Hybrid	Wrightbus Gemini 2	H45/26F	4/13	
20004/13	MX06 BPE/K	Optare M850SL	Optare	B28F	11/13	57
20810/1	BX56 BKA/JZ	Optare M850SL	Optare	B28F	12/13, 11/13	57

Notes

Seating arrangements are shown as originally received/acquired.

Fleet numbers are as originally allotted.

c   Indicates fitted with a torque convertor when new.

O   Indicates built with an open staircase at the back.

%   Sub-contracted out from Leyland Motors.

≠   Rebuilds of PD2/10s with same fleet numbers.

Notes Continued

1. Leyland SG7s Nos. 55/6/9 were reseated to B32D from 1/29.
2. Leyland Leviathans Nos. 63-5 were later fitted with pneumatic tyres and re-designated PLSP1 and PLSP2.
3. Leyland TD3c No. 10 was constructed with an all-metal body and was new in 2/35; No. 4 was written off following an accident on 5th April 1935; No. 1 received the body from No. 9 in -/51.
4. Leyland TD3cs Nos. 2, 5, 8, 10 were reseated with longitudinal seats on the lower deck (L27/26R) in 7/40 to increase the standing capacity.
5. Leyland TD4cs Nos. 11-4, TD2 No. 53, TD3c No. 61 and LT7cs Nos. 81/2 were constructed with all-metal bodies.
6. The following TDs were reseated; No. 11 to H30/26R in 10/51; Nos. 34/5/7/8/9, 40 to H30/26R in 3/52, 6/54, 6/52, 5/52, 1/53 and 1/52; Nos. 41/3/6 to H29/25R by 1/46, -/51 and by 1/46; No. 54 to H30/24R in 9/46, Nos. 62/4 to H30/26R in 7/52 and 9/51 respectively.
7. Leyland TD2 No. 50 was H27/24R.
8. Leyland TD1 No. 60 and TD3c No. 61 were acquired from Leyland Motors.
9. Leyland TD2 No. 69 was H29/24R and No. 70 was H26/24R.
10. Leyland LT5s Nos. 76/9 and TS4 No. 80 were reseated to B28R with perimeter seating in 1/42; No. 80 reverted to B32R in 10/45 and was decorated with light bulbs for National Child Safety Week in March 1950.
11. RN8887 was a replacement for TD3c CK 4924.
12. Leyland PD1s Nos. 60/6 and PD1A No. 106 were renumbered to 8, 12, and 6 in 3/58, 8/58 and 4/57 respectively.
13. Leyland PS1 chassis built in 1946 and stored due to body builders capacity problems; seating capacity reduced to B34F by 7/52.
14. Leyland PD1A No. 91 was reseated to H32/27R in 1959.
15. Leyland PD1A No. 106(6) was written off following an accident at the 'danger bridge' on 18th March 1960 and rebuilt as a breakdown vehicle.
16. The following PD2/10s were reseated between 1959 and 1962; Nos. 20-3, 30 to H32/29R, Nos. 24-9, 31-7 to H33/29R, Nos. 41-51/3/4/7/9, 61 to H32/29R, Nos. 79-83 to H33/29R.
17. Leyland PD2/1 No. 110 was written off following an accident with Crossley-bodied PD2/10 No. 25 on 28th May 1967.
18. Leyland PD3/5 No. 67 was later converted to a PD3/4.
19. The ex-Midland Red Leyland Panthers were renumbered to 237-41 in 5/72; they were reseated to B47D between 2/80 & 4/80.
20. Leyland Panthers Nos. 230-6 were originally registered NRN 230-6K; No. 236 didn't enter service until 4/73; Nos. 233/5/6 were renumbered to 33/5/6 on 30/10/83.
21. Bristol LHSs Nos. 242-4 were renumbered to 342-4 on 17/4/77 and to 42-4 on 30/10/83.
22. Leyland Atlantean No. 115 was loaned to East Staffordshire District Council from 27/5/79 to 4/7/79.
23. Leyland Atlantean No. 134 was initially used by East Lancashire Coachbuilders as a demonstrator.
24. Leyland Atlanteans No. 141-50 were rebuilt to H49/36F between 6/91 and 2/93.
25. Leyland Atlanteans No. 151-77 were rebuilt to H50/36F between 2/90 and 6/93; No. 176 carried two commemorative liveries from 9/98.
26. Leyland Atlanteans Nos.1, 2 were renumbered to 181/2 on 22/11/94; 182 was renumbered to 180 on 23/8/00; they were reseated to H49/29F in 9/94 and 6/94 respectively and re-registered to XEC 415/21Y when sold to Lloyd.
27. Leyland Olympian No. 3 was renumbered to 33 on 22/2/85 and to 133 on 31/3/95 and was originally used as a demonstrator by Leyland Vehicles; reseated to H47/25F in 10/93.
28. Leyland Nationals No. 5-8 were acquired from Merseyside PTE in 8/86; No. 6 was written off following an accident on 10th July 1987.
29. Dodge mini-buses Nos. 6-9 were acquired from Magicbus, Stagecoach Cumberland, Stagecoach Ribble and Magicbus respectively.
30. Leyland Tiger No. 40 was renumbered to 309 on 7/3/95 and re-registered PRN 909 in 12/94.
31. The following Dodge mini-buses were reseated; No. 44 to B22F in 10/87, No. 67 to B20F in 1/94 and Nos. 70/1 to DP22F in 9/95 and 10/95 respectively.

32. Dodge mini-buses Nos. 51/4 were renumbered to 510/40 on 30/11/01.
33. Renault mini-buses Nos. 91/2 were both written off following accidents on 11th January 2001 and 1st October 1999 respectively.
34. Leyland Lynx Nos. 10-13 were renumbered to 210-3 on 15/2/95; 13/2/95; 14/3/95; 7/2/95 respectively.
35. Leyland Lynx Nos. 14-18 were renumbered to 214-8 on 7/2/95; 7/2/95; 8/2/95; 13/2/95; 13/2/95 respectively; No. 215 was reseated to DP49F and fitted with seat belts in 3/05.
36. Leyland Lynx Nos. 219-22 were acquired from Halton Borough Transport Ltd.
37. Leyland Lynx Nos. 23/4/6-9 were renumbered to 223/4/6-9 on 8/2/95; 1/3/95; 13/2/95; 15/2/95; 7/2/95; 15/2/95 respectively.
38. Leyland Olympians No. 32 was renumbered to 132 on 8/2/95 and to 100 on 10/2/05.
39. Leyland Olympians Nos. 34-7 were renumbered to 134-7 on 17/3/95; 7/4/95; 1/4/95; 12/4/95 respectively.
40. Leyland Olympian No. 106 was originally a demonstrator for Leyland Vehicles.
41. Leyland Olympian No. 107 was received in a special livery for the 1992 Guild and was fitted with LED destination equipment under Stagecoach ownership.
42. Leyland Olympian No. 110 was used to trial a new livery arrangement for the Tridents; Nos. 108/9 (42558/9) wore a special livery for the 2012 Guild.
43. Optare Metroriders Nos. 1-4, 39 and 40 were branded for Park & Ride services.
44. Optare Metrorider No. 18 was written off following an accident on 30th April 2008.
45. Optare Metroriders Nos. 41/2 were acquired from Blackburn Transport.
46. Dennis Tridents Nos. 182-8 were route branded for services 22 & 23; fitted with LED destination equipment in 2011-4.
47. Dennis Tridents Nos. 190-6 were route branded for services 33 & 35; fitted with LED destination equipment in 2011-3.
48. Volvo B10M No. 323 was re-registered PRN 909 on 10/3/03 and back to T894 HBF on 13/7/06.
49. Leyland Olympians Nos. 123-32 were acquired from Lothian Buses and were rebuilt to H51/34F before entering service; No. 130 was fitted with seat belts in 3/07.
50. Optare Solos Nos. 51-8 were route branded for service 19.
51. Optare Solos Nos. 59-67 and Solo SRs Nos. 1-8 were delivered in a special Park & Ride colour scheme; No. 61 was fitted with a plaque behind the driver's cab declaring it to be the 1000th Solo built.
52. Scanias Nos. 203-7 were originally registered PL06 RYR/T/U/V/W and were re-registered before entering service.
53. Dennis Tridents 18540-4 were acquired from Lothian Buses and fitted with LED destination equipment.
54. Former Wrightbus demonstrators; Nos. 20907/9 were reseated to B33F in 10/12.
55. Optare Versa No. 30128 was received with Black Diamond logo seats which were changed after a few weeks and was renumbered to 30131 on 18/7/12.
56. Dennis Tridents 40600/1 were acquired from Stagecoach London via Ensignbus and fitted with LED destination equipment.
57. Transferred from Rotala Diamond.

Services operated as at 30th September 1948

Route	Destination	Notes
A	Town Centre (Harris Street) to Ashton Pedders Lane	
B	Town Centre (Corporation Street) to Ashton Inkerman Street	
BR	Town Centre (Birley Street) to Broadgate	Linked with the FP
C	Town Centre (Harris Street) to Lane Ends Ashton	Linked with the HS
D	Fulwood Circular via Deepdale	Town Centre bus stop in Lancaster Road
F	Fulwood Circular via North Road	Town Centre bus stop in Lancaster Road
FP	Town Centre (Church Street) to Farringdon Park	Linked with the BR
FR	Town Centre (Lancaster Road) to Fulwood Row	Certain journeys extended to Long Sand Lane
GL	Town Centre (Church Street) to Ribbleton Gamull Lane	Interworked with the P5
HS	Town Centre (Jacson Street) to Holme Slack	Linked with the C
LEC	Cemetery to Ashton Pedders Lane	Sundays pm only
M	Town Centre (Church Street) to Moorside	
R	Town Centre (Church Street) to Ribbleton Chatburn Road	Limited Service
PL	Town Centre (Birley Street) to Boys Lane or Queens Drive	
P1	Frenchwood to / from Lea Victoria Park Drive	Joint with Ribble MS / Scout MS; via Town Centre
P2	Fulwood Lightfoot Lane to / from Penwortham Plough Inn	Joint with Ribble MS / Scout MS; via Town Centre
P5	Hutton Anchor Inn to / from Ribbleton Gamull Lane	Joint with Ribble MS / Scout MS; interworked with the GL; via Town Centre

Services operated as at 31st May 1989

Route	Destination	Notes
3	Longton	Mon-Sat
4	Penwortham	Limited number of journeys routed via Broadgate
5	Brookfield via Cromwell Road	Mon-Sat
6	Brookfield via Deepdale	Mon-Sat
7	Fulwood Row via Garstang Road	
8	Moor Nook via Ribbleton Avenue	
11	Ribbleton Gamull Lane	
14	Holme Slack	Evenings & Sundays excepted
16	Farringdon Park	
17	Bamber Bridge	
19	Royal Preston Hospital via Deepdale	
21	Broadgate	Mon-Sat
22	Fulwood (RPH) via Plungington Road	Evenings & Sundays excepted

Services operated as at 31st May 1989 continued

23	Fulwood Asda via Plungington Road	Early am, evenings & Sundays excepted
24	Lea via Hawthorn Crescent	Mon-Sat
25	Lea via Tulketh Road	
26	Lea via Waterloo Road	Limited Service on Mon-Fri
27	Larches Estate via Tulketh Brow	
29	Frenchwood	
30	Savick Estate (via Fylde Road & Mariners Way)	Sunday Service routed via Tulketh Road vice Mariners Way
31	Broughton & Woodplumpton	Limited Service on Mon-Fri
32	Tanterton via Lightfoot Lane	
33	Tanterton via Brook Street	
34	Ingol via Fylde Road	Evenings & Sundays excepted
43	Ingol via Mill Lane	Mon-Sat
44	Ingol via Brook Street	Early am, evenings & Sundays only
98	Cemetery to Ashton Lane Ends	One journey only on Mon-Fri early am
99	Moor Nook to Royal Preston Hospital	Limited Service early am
114	Holme Slack Fairfax Road	Interworked with the 14
123	Sherwood via Plungington Road	Early am, evenings & Sundays only; interworked with the 23
126	Clayton Green Asda	Limited Service
127	Lea & Larches Estate	Limited Service on Mon-Sat; interworked with the 27
184†	Salwick	Limited Service on Mon-Sat

Services operated as at 31st May 2013

Route	Destination	Notes
1†	Capitol Centre to Portway (Park & Ride)	Mon-Sat
3A†	Broadgate	Mon-Sat evenings excepted
4B†	Fulwood Circular	Mon-Sat
8	Moor Nook via Ribbleton Avenue	
12†	Longton via Penwortham	Mon-Sat
12A†	Longton via Broadgate & Penwortham	One inbound evening journey on Mon-Sat
13†	Penwortham via Lower Penwortham	Mon-Sat
13A†	Penwortham via Broadgate & Lower Penwortham	Mon-Sat
14	Brookfield via Holme Slack	Evening & Sun worked by Stagecoach to Fairfax Rd
16	Farringdon Park	
19	Royal Preston Hospital via Deepdale & Broadwood Drive	Limited Service on Mon-Sat
19A	Royal Preston Hospital via Deepdale	
22	Royal Preston Hospital via Plungington Road	Limited Service on Mon-Fri
23	Fulwood Asda via Plungington Road	
31	Lea via Savick	
31A	Lea via Savick & Hawthorn Crescent	Mon-Sat evenings excepted
35	Tanterton via Fylde Road	
44	Ingol via Plungington Road	Mon-Sat
68†	Blackpool via Lytham & St Annes	Sun-Thu evening only
86	Royal Preston Hospital via Brookfield	Sundays only
88A	Orbit Anti-clockwise	Mon-Sat
88C	Orbit Clockwise	Mon-Sat
89	Lea / Larches via Railway Station	Limited Service to Lea on Mon-Fri
112†	Croston via Frenchwood & Leyland	Mon-Sat
113†	Wigan via Leyland & Eccleston	Mon-Sat evenings only
114†	Chorley via Frenchwood & Lostock Hall	Mon-Sat
119	Royal Preston Hospital via Deepdale & Preston College	Limited Service on school days
†	Service operated under contract to Lancashire County Council	
	All services operated from the Bus Station except the Park & Ride	

Trams operated 1904-1935

No.	Builder	Trucks	Motors	Seating	Date
1-26	ER & TCW	Brill 21E	DK25A	O26/22	6/04
27-30	ER & TCW	Brill 22E	DK34A	O38/30	6/04
31-3	UEC Co	Brill 39E	DK9A3	40	9/12
34-9	UEC Co	Brill 21E	DK9A3	30/22	-/14
40-5†	ER & TCW	Brill 21E	DK25A	28	11/19
46-8†	Brush	Brill 21E	DK25A	28	-/20
40	EE Co/PCTD	Preston Std	DK94/1C	40/22	-/28
42*	EE Co/PCTD	Preston Std	DK94/1C	40/22	-/29
13/8, 22≠	EE Co	Brill 21E	DK30B	30/22	7/29

ER & TCW	Electric Railway & Tramway Carriage Works.
UEC Co	United Electric Car Company.
EE Co	English Electric Company.
PCTD	Preston Corporation Transport Department.
*	Standard No. 42 was renumbered 30 in 1932.
†	Bought from Sheffield Corporation in 1919/20; Nos. 41/3-8 –were renumbered using vacant numbers between 1-28 in 1932.
≠	Bought from Lincoln Corporation in 1929.

Preston Area Map

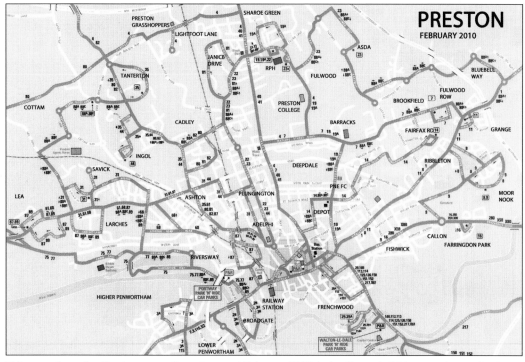

This map shows the Preston area with routes as at February 2010 during the period Stagecoach were in charge of operations, shortly before the routes reverted to the pre-Stagecoach network.

This scene typifies the fate which befell most of the Corporation's 63 PD2s. Apart from the eight Rebuilds only a handful managed to escape the cutters torch after their service in Preston. 1955 MCW-bodied Leyland PD2/10 No. 80 is only days away from its final demise in G Jones scrapyard at Carlton on the outskirts of Barnsley. Having been

the first of the quintet to be withdrawn in April 1976 it languished in the garage yard for a whole year before being towed away on 22nd April 1977. This view was taken four days later. Nos. 81-3 of the same batch had all departed Deepdale on the 16th and their remains were also present in the yard. No. 79 initially found use as a Promotional Vehicle with Jeff Brownhut and managed to eke out another seven years before being disposed of to Parton & Allen, another of the Barnsley breakers.